"Eclipse"

Osiefield Anderson, Ph.D.

©2011 by Dr. Osiefield Anderson, Ph.D. and Gregory Anderson. All rights are reserved.

No part of this book may be reproduced, stored in a retrieval system, or transmitted by any means without the written permission of the author.

Published by Dr. Osiefield Anderson, Ph.D. (2/2011)

ISBN: -13: 978-1500138257

ISBN: -10: 1500138258

Acknowledgement

To God

Be The

Glory!

Osiefield Anderson, Ph.D

Preface

Eclipse is a very interesting account of a white couple (John and Patricia Smith) who has amassed lots of wealth. John is a tycoon!

John and Patricia are living a life of eutopian delight. However, one thing is missing – they have not been blessed with a child. John and Patricia are Christians and believe in the Biblical Passage: "To everything there is a season, and a time to every purpose under the heaven" (Ecc. 3:1). This is their faith; this is there hope! After fifteen years of marriage, their season comes and Patricia is pregnant. They are exhilarated! The good news is announced in their Church, and they give a lavish party in celebration of their forthcoming son!

It seems like many lifetimes, but the day of delivery finally comes. John is in the Waiting Room waiting for the good news. He is taken to see his wife and son and discovers that his son is Black! John is hysterical and declares that he is not the father of a Black child. He accuses Patricia of having an affair with a Negro, but the results of three DNA tests declare that he (John) is the baby's father. Despite the DNA tests, John contends that he is not the baby's father and this causes a schism in the family. However, as the story unfolds, unbeknownst to John, he employs his son as CEO of the Home Branch of his (John's) Enterprise.

The Book is written in playwright format to give the characters in the Book a real-life effect, to make the

Preface (Cont'd)

drama unfold more naturally, and to make the Book more interesting to read.

Eclipse

John and Patricia Smith is a white couple that has amassed millions in wealth. They are a happy couple with one missing link – they have not been blessed with a child. Patricia (Pat) is disappointed, but John is disturbed. The scene opens and they are in conference with their Pastor, The Reverend Dr. Mike Champion, of St. Peters Baptist Church, Robinsonville, Virginia.

DR. CHAMPION

John, I certainly can understand your concerns. Most couples want a child. It's normal! But these matters over which we have little or no control don't always happen on our schedule, and we have to be patient.

John jumps up from his chair and shouts –

JOHN

Are you kidding, Pastor Champion? Did you say, patient?

Looking at Patricia, John exclaims –

JOHN (CONT'D)

Pat and I have been married fifteen years, Pastor, and you say, "Be Patient!"

Patricia gets up, walks up to John, smiles, as she looks straight into his eyes and gives him a hug and says –

PATRICIA

John, Honey, calm yourself! It's going to be all right! As badly as we want a child, let's be thankful that we have each other- until "death do we part!"

John calms down a bit and exclaims –

JOHN

Sorry, Pastor Champion – Sorry, I got upset.

DR. CHAMPION

That's ok, John. I know exactly how you feel.

Much more calmly now, John responds –

JOHN

But how could you possibly know how Pat and I feel – you have three children?

It's silent for a few moments and Dr. Champion responds –

DR. CHAMPION

Yes, you are right, John, we do have three kids. But what you don't know and even Milissa, our oldest
don't know, is that she is adopted.

It's silent for more than a minute and Patricia says –

PATRICIA

Oh, Pastor, we are so sorry!

DR. CHAMPION

No, Pat, there's nothing to be sorry about. Milissa was a blessing from God.

JOHN

Don't quite follow you, Pastor. I know you and Mrs. Champion love her and

Dr. Champion interrupts –

DR. CHAMPION

It's more than that, John. You see Peg (Mrs. Champion) and I were somewhat like Abraham and Sarah. We sort of held God responsible for our not having that baby boy that we so desperately longed for. But after we adopted Milissa, just a little more than a year later, Peg was pregnant and then God blessed us with Mike, Jr. and two years later, Cassandra.

JOHN

Gee, Pastor Champion, I can see. Maybe, subconsciously, I have been faulting God, too.

PATRICIA

You see, Pastor, John and I have had tests after tests and according to the tests there is absolutely

PATRICIA (CONT'D)

no reason that I haven't gotten pregnant!

DR. CHAMPION

The two of you just be prayerfully patient, and it will be ok. Remember Paul has assured us that, "Let us not be weary in well-doing: For in due season we shall reap, if we faint not" (Galatians 6:9).

JOHN

Well said, Pastor Champion.

Looking at Patricia, John smiles and says –

JOHN (CONT'D)

We're going to make it! We got each other and that's
our ticket to anywhere we want to go!

Dr. Champion stands and with a big smile says -

DR. CHAMPION

That seems like a winner to me –

Patricia, with a glow of joy and satisfaction in her eyes , joyfully exclaims –

PATRICIA

Bingo!

Patricia and John shake hands with Dr. Champion and leave his office. The scene closes and opens three months later. John opens the door to their mansion and yells –

JOHN

The aroma of delicious food is permeating the air, but
De De (the maid) isn't around! Who's here?

Patricia yells back –

PATRICIA

Come on back to the den of lions!

JOHN

All right by me, because Daniel is in me and the lions will be my pillows of comfort and rest!

Patricia jumps up with smiles all over her pretty face and says –

PATRICIA

Guess who I am, Dear!

JOHN

The pretty, sweet and wonderful….and lover of the luckiest man in all the world –ME!

PATRICIA

Amen! Amen! Amen, Brother!

John and Patricia embrace and the atmosphere is full of joy, hope and a benediction too deep for words can be felt!

JOHN

Where is De De? Did you fire her?

PATRICIA

No, no, Dear! I decided to prepare the meal so I could have you all by myself – so, I gave her the day off!

JOHN

That's fine by me! But what's up?

PATRICIA

Naturally, as usual, you are hungry. So, let me feed you, Dear, then I will reveal my secret! I have planned an excursion for us.

JOHN

We've been all over the world, and I didn't know that trips to the moon were already available!

PATRCIA

Lots you don't know, my Dear John! Lots!

The scene closes and opens as John and Patricia finish their meal and John says –

JOHN

Since you gave De De the day off, I surmise that I'm to help you with the dishes.

PATRICIA

That's the spirit, my dear – That's the spirit!

While taking care of the dishes, Patricia is constantly smiling and tranquility can be seen in everything she does and in everything she says. John comments –

JOHN

Pat, I have a feeling that this excursion is not the main issue – let the "cat out of the bag."

PATRICIA

Ok, daddy, then what is it?

It's quiet for a few moments and Patricia says, quietly –

PATRICIA (CONT'D)

Ok, then what is it, Daddy?

John stretches his eyes and yells –

JOHN

Pat, you called me Daddy!

With hands raised in exultation, John jumps up from his chair and, simultaneously, Pat does also and Pat says –

PATRICIA

Yes, dear, I am two months pregnant! Two months!

John runs around the room, knocking over chairs and shouting!

JOHN

Daddy! Daddy! What music! Why did you wait so long to tell me?

PATRICIA

We, Dr. Pace and I, wanted to be absolutely certain and beyond any possible doubt. We knew it would be too painful to tell you that I was pregnant and later tell you it was a mistake!

The scene closes and opens to John and Patricia embraced and dancing to: Misty Blue. The scene depicts them dancing, smiling and occasionally kissing. The scene closing and opens and John is seen getting off his knees in prayer and says to Patricia –

JOHN

Pat, God has answered our prayer –

PATRICIA

Yes, he has John! Yes, he has!

Patricia lifts her arms as gazing up to heaven and says –

PATRICIA (CONT'D)

Is there anything too hard for God?

JOHN

Pat, we are going to have a big celebration – that's right – a gigantic celebration.

John raises his hand and yells –

JOHN (CONT'D)

Got an idea, Pat – yes, an idea!

PATRICIA

And what is this "earth shaking" idea, John?

JOHN

My dad's first name is James and your dad's first name is Julian and, being the only children, they are longing for a grandson, so we are going to call our son J.J., for James and Julian. How about that?

PATRICIA

Sounds good to me!

The scene closes and John and Patricia are visiting Dr. Champion, their Pastor.

DR. CHAMPION

Well, Abraham and Sarah, now we can answer that question: Is there anything too hard for God? The answer is, No!

JOHN

And that's for sure, Pastor Champion. This calls for a celebration.

DR. CHAMPION

A celebration! Well, I think we should say, an extended celebration!

PATRICIA

I know that's right, Pastor!

The scene closes and opens at the "Bananza Plaza" in Marshalville Heights, a Suburban of Robinsonville. It's a "gala affair" in honor of The Smith's baby to be born. The MC (Bob Tate, CEO of Atomic Industries) is speaking –

BOB

Ladies and Gentlemen, this occasion is second only to the Queen's visit with Solomon. She was so startled that what she beholds is far greater than that she heard about Solomon's wisdom and riches. So she exclaimed: "The half ain't never been told!" Tonight, we celebrate fifteen years of hoping, praying and waiting for

Looking and pointing to John and Patricia –

BOB (CONT'D)

the birth of the child of my closest and dearest friends – John and Patricia Smith.

Everyone stands and applauds for seems like an eternity. Then Bob continues –

BOB (CONT'D)

Ladies and Gentlemen, to get us off to a good start tonight, Pastor, Dr. Mike Champion, of the St. Peters Baptist Church is here. Let's hear him.

The audience stands and applauds as Pastor Champion walks to the podium –

DR. CHAMPION

Ladies and gents, this is a moment of spiritual triumph, not only for John and Pat Smith, but for each of us. We cannot always know when our "tomorrow" will come nor its status. We must learn to trust God, Whose Wisdom far transcends ours infinitely millions of times. But, this we know: "To everything is a season, and a time to every purpose under the heaven" (Eccl. 3:1).

Dr. Champion looks at John and Patricia and says –

DR. CHAMPION (CONT'D)

To you, my dear Friends, your season has come. Be thankful; be grateful; be humble; be blessed. As little as we might know, God only wants the best for His children – And we are His children. Let this be a night of thanksgiving! Let this be a night of praise; let this be a night of searching our hearts and minds to see what we are going to say to God, Thank you! Amen!

The scene depicts a festivity that has to be admired by angels. The scene closes and John and Patricia are enroute home. John parks at a nearby baseball stadium near their home. John says –

JOHN

Pat, this has been a delightful night of both human and angelic splendor! Indeed, I am grateful to those who came out to join us in our celebration. But most of all, I thank God for letting it be!

Patricia, wiping tears of joy, exclaims –

PATRICIA

Amen! Amen! Amen!

The scene closes and opens several months later, and John and Patricia are in the "Delivery Room." John looks at Patricia, raises his right hand and uses the appropriate fingers and makes the letter "V," and says to Pat –

JOHN

> V-Day, Honey!

Patricia smiles and gives him (John) the "thumb upper" sign! Dr. Parks and Nurse Meeks enter the room and Dr. Parks says to John and Patricia –

DR. PARKS

> To avoid any risk of inflicting any harm to your baby boy, it is determined that Mrs. Smith should have a caesarean birth. As you know, this is simply routine!

A team of nurses and assistants wheel Patricia into the room for the caesarean birth. The scene closes and opens, Patricia has come out of the effect of the anesthesia and awaiting to see her baby boy. Finally, Nurse Meeks comes to Patricia, handing her baby to her and says –

NURSE MEEKS

> Mrs. Smith, here's your healthy baby boy!

Patricia screams –

PATRICIA

> Oh No! Oh, No! There must be a mistake; This is a black baby! Oh, No!

The shock causes Patricia to pass out, Nurse Meeks calls for Dr. Parks who enters the room and they are in the process of reviving Patricia.

> DR. PARKS

Mrs. Smith, I can understand the shock, but lots of white couples adopt Black and children of other races.

> PATRICIA

Dr. There must be some mistake. How can I explain this to my husband!

> DR. PARKS

There's nothing to explain!

The scene closes and opens and Dr. Parks walks into the Waiting Room where John is waiting to hear the good news. John is pacing the floor when Dr. Parks enters the room and says –

> JOHN

Dr. is Pat ok?

> DR. PARKS

Oh, yes, Mr. Smith, she is fine!

> JOHN

And the baby?

                    DR. PARKS

    Oh, he's fine, but –

John interrupts –

                    JOHN

    Let me see them.

                    DR. PARKS

    Ok, Mr. Smith, but I wanted to explain –

John interrupts again and says –

                    JOHN

    Dr. Just let me see my wife and my son. You can explain whatever it is later.

The scene closes as Dr. Parks and John are leaving the Waiting Room to go to the room in which Patricia is housed. As Dr. Parks and John enter the room, John can see that Patricia is crying. He rushes to her side, embraces her and says –

                    JOHN

    It's ok Honey, the baby is fine – what's wrong? Why are you crying?

Patricia begins to scream –

PATRICIA

John, Honey, I am so sorry! Honey, I am so sorry!

John looks at Dr. Parks and says –

JOHN

Dr. somebody tell me what's wrong!

Dr. Parks takes the baby and takes off the blanket and hands the baby to John. John looks in amazement and remarks –

JOHN

Whose baby is this? Where is my baby?

DR. PARKS

Mr. Smith, this is your baby.

JOHN

The hell it is! There must be some mistake, my wife and I are both white and this baby is Black. Is this some kind of Halloween Prank?

DR. PARKS

Mr. Smith, I can understand your being surprised to have a Black baby, but this is a professional business and we simply cannot have this kind of commotion.

John settles down a bit and reacts more calmly.

JOHN

Dr. Parks, I apologize for my irrational behavior, but I demand that somebody does a DNA on this baby to verify my claim that I'm not the father.

DR. PARKS

Indeed, that's your right. We will have one done immediately.

The scene closes and opens as a DNA is being done. In the meantime, John is talking to Patricia –

JOHN

Pat, all I ask you to do is come clean with me! You must have been involved with some Black man and this has to be his baby!

Patricia just stares for a few moments and responds –

PATRICIA

John, as I think about it, if I were you and you were me, I think that I, too, might find it difficult to believe you. It's in your mind that I have not only been unfaithful to you but with a Black man. It would no doubt be much easier and less painful for me to lie and say I had an affair with some Black man and our baby – yes, yours and mine, is his baby. But, I won't lie about the truth!

JOHN

Pat, it might hurt, but I can accept and live with the truth, but how can I live with a lie?

PATRICIA

John, I have told you the truth! What you believe is your concern!

The scene closes and opens as Dr. Parks enters the room with the DNA results and John jumps up and exclaims –

JOHN

Dr. Parks, now tell me if I am not right!

Dr. Parks looks at John and retorts –

DR. PARKS

Mr. Smith, oftentimes, the truth is in the mind of the believer.

Holding up the results, Dr. Parks says –

DR. PARKS (CONT'D)

According to the DNA results, Mr. Smith, as strangely as it might seems, you are the baby's father!

John goes into a rage again –

JOHN

There has to be some mistake in this DNA report – who did it – I demand that it is done again and by some neutral firm.

DR. PARKS

Fine, Sir. Have anybody you want to do it, but the results will be the same.

John insists that several DNA tests be done and each one comes back and confirms that he (John) is the baby's father. The scene closes and opens and John is in conversation with Dr. Champion, his Pastor.

DR. CHAMPION

John, my Boy, I know how you must feel –

John cuts in –

JOHN

I appreciate your concerns, Pastor, but unless you have worn my moccasins, you cannot possibly know how I feel.

DR. CHAMPION

If what you say were true, then a male pediatrician cannot know the pain that some mothers have giving birth. I have three children and, except for Milissa, my adopted child, I am certain I know how I would feel to certainly learn

DR. CHAMPION (CONT'D)

that the other two are not mine. The main problem John is that you don't want to believe that you are the baby's father.

JOHN

And why not?

DR. CHAMPION

It lessens the guilt of divorcing Pat.

JOHN

Pat will be ok. She will have more than enough money for her and her child to live comfortably.

DR. CHAMPION

John, John, do you think - for one moment - that money is what's on Pat's mind? Of course not!

It's silent for a few moments and John says –

JOHN

Well, Pastor Champion, I have to do what I have to do –

DR. CHAMPION

John, you are searching to find just one person who agrees with you and I can tell from your talk that you haven't found one, including yourself.

The scene closes. John parents, Mr. and Mrs. James Smith of Tucan, Georgia, are standing by the phone waiting to hear the good news about the delivery of their grandson. The scene opens as John is talking to Patricia –

JOHN

What on earth will I tell mama and daddy?

PATRICIA

Just tell them the truth, John.

JOHN

Pat, I don't know the truth! The only truth I know is that I am a white man and you are a white woman and we are supposed to believe that we are the parents of a black baby! God forbids!

Finally, John's father calls and John recognizes that number and won't answer. Patricia can tell from John's expression who the caller is and says

PATRICIA

John, I know that's your daddy! Talk to him.

JOHN

About what? Do you think, for one minute, that daddy is going to believe that his grandson is a black child?

PATRICIA

He can believe whatever he wants to, the fact of the matter is that this is his grandson!

Mr. Smith turns to talk with his wife Teresa –

MR. SMITH

Resa, something is wrong! I know it!

MRS. SMITH

Well, James, what on earth could it be – you reckon anything is wrong with the baby?

MR. SMITH

I don't know, but I know that my boy wouldn't let his phone ring off the hook without answering it if everything is ok –

MRS. SMITH

James, call the Delivery Room and try to see if they know something we don't!

MR. SMITH

Good idea, Resa.

Mr. Smith dials information to get the number –

INFORMATION

This is Information! May I help you?

MR. SMITH

Yes, please give me the number to the Delivery Room of Holy Cross Hospital in Robinsville.

INFORMATION

Yes, Sir. The number is (821) 263-1111.

MR. SMITH

Thanks!

Mr. Smith immediately begins to dial the number. The phone answers.

ATTENDANT

Delivery! May I help you?

MR. SMITH

This is James Smith, my son's wife is or has given birth to a baby boy and I cannot get in touch with my son, John Smith.

ATTENDANT

Yes, Sir. Hold for a moment, please!

There are a few moments of waiting and the Attendant responds –

ATTENDANT

Sir, the baby has been delivered and is doing fine.

MR. SMITH

Then why on earth won't my son answer his phone?

ATTENDANT

Sir, there seems to be a slight problem.

MR. SMITH

What kind of a slight problem?

ATTENDANT

Child Identity.

MR. SMITH

Mam, what on earth do you mean – child identity!

ATTENDANT

Sir, let me give your son a message –

MR. SMITH

Good! Tell him to answer his damn phone. His mama and I are sitting on pins and needles.

ATTENDANT

Very well, Sir.

The attendant hangs up and goes to John and says –

ATTENDANT (CONT'D)

Mr. Smith, I have an urgent message from your father! He says that you won't answer your phone and he and your mother are on pins and needles! Please call them!

Patricia hears the Attendant and says –

PATRICIA

John, be a man and call your mama and daddy!

JOHN

And what am I to tell them – that their grandson is a black child?

PATRICIA

John, you are beginning to sound like a broken record! Tell them what it is – not telling them is not going to change one thing! Not one thing!

John doesn't respond to his father. Mr. Smith looks at Mrs. Smith, hangs up the phone and says –

MR. SMITH

Resa, let's go down there and see what on earth is wrong!

MRS. SMITH

I guess we should!

Mr. Smith calls Patricia's parents –

MRS. SMITH

Matilda, this is Teresa. Have you and Julian heard anything from Pat and John. He simply refuses to talk to us.

MRS. FOXX

Hey, Teresa, no Jul and I haven't heard a word. We know that Pat would not be really in a position, but we thought John would have called.

MRS. SMITH

Well, James and I are on our way to the hospital.

MRS. FOXX

Good, Jul and I will meet you all there.

The scene closes and opens and The Smiths and Foxx's are in the parking lot of the hospital.

MR. SMITH

Julian, I am as confused as a bat at "high noon!" Don't have the slightest idea as to what's going on!

MR. FOXX

Neither do I. Let's go on in and find out what's going on.

The Smiths and Foxx's go into the hospital and get information and go directly to where John and Pat are. They can see that John is hysterical and his father, Mr. Smith, walks over to him and says –

MR. SMITH

John, what on earth are you so upset about, boy!

John raises his hands above his head and says –

JOHN

Daddy, all hell has broken loose! It's horrible!

MR. SMITH

What's horrible? Make sense, Son! Settle down, Son!

John shakes his hands and says –

JOHN

Ok, Daddy, ok!

MR. SMITH

Good! Now tell us what is the problem.

JOHN

Daddy, I don't know how to tell you all this, but the baby is black!

Both parents are awestruck and Mr. Smith says –

MR. SMITH

Calm yourself, Son! There has to be some mistake!

JOHN

I wish it were!

MR. FOXX

What do you mean, you wish it were – there has to be a mistake! There just has to be!

JOHN

We have had three DNA tests and they all are negative – but I refuse to believe that I am the father of a black baby.

MR. SMITH

And you aren't! Just hold on!

The Attendant on duty says to the families – talking to Mr. Smith –

ATTENDANT

Sir, it would be better if you all went down to a Conference Room where you all can be alone and discuss this matter.

MR. SMITH

Good idea! Please direct us to one.

The Attendant takes them down to a Conference Room

ATTENDANT

Here we are, Sir. You can go in there and have privacy to discuss the matter.

and, looking, Mr. Smith says –

MR. SMITH

Thanks, Mam!

The scene fast-forwards to the conclusion of their discussion about the baby and Mr. Smith looks at Mrs. Smith and Mrs. Foxx and exclaims –

MR. SMITH

What about you grandmama hopefuls? Don't you have something to say?

MRS. SMITH

I am sure that we do, but you two have been in such an uproar that we couldn't get in a word if we tried.

It's silent for a few moments and Mrs. Smith says –

MRS. SMITH (CONT'D)

I can clearly understand the shockness that all of us are realizing, but what about that poor child lying in there – Patricia?

Mrs. Foxx is weeping and says –

MRS. FOXX

That's right Teresa! Only God know that agony that she must be having, and we are not making thing any better – but worse!

JOHN

And what are we supposed to do? I have been waiting, seemingly a life-time, for a boy and this –

MRS. SMITH

I tell you, John, we are supposed to act like adults – grown-ups and not like some irrational juveniles.

JOHN

Mama, if the child had come here abnormal I could understand and accept it, but

Mrs. Smith interrupts John and says –

MRS. SMITH

Hold it! Hold it, John! Are you saying that a child is better off to be abnormal than black?

JOHN

Yes, if the child is born to a white family!

Dr. Champion has joined the group and comments –

DR. CHAMPION

Are you aware, John that some white couples have adopted black children?

It's quiet for a few moments and John responds –

JOHN

Well, that was by choice.

John looks at his parents and then to Pat's parents and says –

JOHN (CONT'D)

Tell me mama, and you, too, Mrs. Foxx, if either Pat or I had been born black, would you have accepted us?

MRS. SMITH

It's difficult or really impossible for anyone to say what he would have done under circumstances he never experienced.

MRS. FOXX

Yes, I agree. But I want John to explain his position – really, tell me, Pat's mother, why you are so stubbornly opposed to any explanation?

JOHN

All right, I will – your daughter, my wife, must have had an affair with a Negro man and got

JOHN (CONT'D)

pregnant for him. There's no other rational explanation!

It's silent for moments, then Mrs. Foxx says,

MRS. FOXX

John, I am sympathetic with your problem, but I refuse to sit here and let you label my daughter as being an unfaithful wife without a shred of evidence.

Mrs. Foxx raises her hands and her voice and says –

MRS. FOXX (CONT'D)

Yes, I know, it's hard to conceive of a white man and a white woman having a black baby, but I believe my daughter.

JOHN

Believe what you will, but I'm out of here!

DR. CHAMPION

Really, John's problem is a social one. He can't bring himself to feel what it would be like to be called daddy by a black child. Even if God Almighty told him that he is that baby's father, he would rebel!

JOHN

Say what you will! I'm out of here!

John rapidly walks out of the door and goes his way. Mrs. Smith remarks –

MRS. SMITH

Why this is trust upon us, I don't know! Let's pray that we will do what is right.

The scene fades as the Mrs. Smith and Mrs. Foxx embrace and Mr. Smith and Mr. Foxx shake hands. The scene closes. The scene opens in Patricia's room; she is in dialogue with her parents, Mr. and Mrs. Julian Foxx –

PATRICIA

Mama, there has to be a message in this ordeal! What hurts me most of all is John's behavior. It's not so much that he distrusts me; he distrusts himself. Yet, I rather that he goes his own way than to stay with my baby and me out of obligation, opposed to love.

The scene closes and opens and Patricia is at home with her parents -

MR. FOXX

Well, Pat, I don't know how, but you got yourself in a helluva mess!

Patricia interrupts and says –

PATRICIA

I can't believe what I'm hearing!

Looking her father in his eyes, Patricia raises her arms and exclaims –

PATRICIA (CONT'D)

I've got myself in a helluva mess! And what on earth have I done. Thanks God, I wasn't born Black!

Mrs. Foxx chimes in –

MRS. FOXX

Julian, I am a bit shocked! Pat is our daughter – our only child – and a child should always be able to find refuge at home! Just what are you inferring?

It's silent for a few moments, then Mr. Foxx says –

MR. FOXX

Til (Matilda) I was just thinking of Pat. This baby just got here and with good adopted parents, he would grow up and never know the difference.

Patricia burst in –

PATRICIA

Maybe he wouldn't, but I would! I regret that I cannot find words of consolation and sound advice from my father.

MRS. FOXX

Pat, I think Julian means well, but hasn't really thought things out.

PATRICIA

Really, mama, there isn't anything to think out!

Pointing to J.J. in his crib, Patricia says –

PATRICIA (CONT'D)

That boy is my baby – my child, mama! I don't know why he came here black. But, he's my black child just as much as he would be if he were "lilly white!" and I am going to keep him and raise him no matter what!

MRS. FOXX

Pat, I am in your corner! And I am glad to hear you say that. And that child is my grandson, and it doesn't matter what's his color.

MR. FOXX

I'm just looking down the road! Is this baby worth the loss of all Pat has to lose to keep him?

MR. FOXX (CONT'D)

You know, John has already taken his position on the matter.

Mr. Foxx raises his arms in desperation and exclaims –

MR. FOXX (CONT'D)

Pat has the world in her hands – a good husband and security - second to none! She's going to lose all of that!

MRS. FOXX

Julian, security is good to have, and I'm glad we have it. But we are not talking about security – we are talking about the well-being of a mother and her child – a mother who loves her child who just happens to be of a different color than hers and her husband's. And that mother happens to be our daughter – yes, yours and mine!

Mr. Foxx gets up and walks into the kitchen, looks in the mirror on the wall and looks and sees Patricia and her mother embracing as Patricia is about to leave. Mr. Foxx yells –

MR. FOXX

Til, you and Pat hold it for a moment!

Patricia turns and says –

PATRICIA

Daddy, I think it's best that I go!

MR. FOXX

Just hold on for a few minutes. I have something I want to say and I think you might just be interested.

Mrs. Foxx and Patricia come back and sit down. Mr. Foxx stands for a few moments and says –

MR. FOXX (CONT'D)

I went in that kitchen to get a glass of wine, and, you know, that damn mirror has been hanging on that wall for years – since Pat was a baby – and not thinking, I looked in that mirror and I was shocked at the man I saw! The man I saw there was a selfish old man who thought life was measured by money, influence, knowing the right people, and countless nothingness. What a tragedy!

Mr. Foxx goes over to the crib and takes out little J.J. and says –

MR. FOXX (CONT'D)

This by is my grandson – yes, our grandson. Just think had Dr. George Washington Carver, Booker T. Washington, Mrs. Mary Mcleod Bethune had been born white and their mothers lacked what it takes, come what may, to have raised them!

Holding little J.J. close to his heart, Mr. Foxx continues –

MR. FOXX (CONT'D)

Pat, you don't know how sorry I am for being so selfish and so stupid! Indeed, you should keep your child. And if John is too much of a weakling to accept his responsibility and duty, you hang in there and your mama and I will be with you each step of the way!

With tears flowing from all their eyes, Patricia embraces her father and the scene closes and opens at a called meeting at St. Peters Baptist Church. Dr. Champion is at the podium –

DR. CHAMPION

Brothers and Sisters, as you know this meeting is called to allow persons of our membership to express their concerns about one of our long-time, standing and faithful members – Pat Smith. I have discussed this issue with members of our Deacon Board and everyone knows my opinion on this matter.

A member, Marcel Bates, raises her hand and Dr. Champion recognizes her –

DR. CHAMPION

Ok, Sister Bates, let us hear your concerns.

MS. BATES

Pastor Champion, I don't think we have any choice but to request that Pat Smith moves her membership!

DR. CHAMPION

And may I ask, Sister Bates, to where would you suggest that Pat moves her membership?

MS. BATES

Well, Pastor Champion, that will be her choice.

DR. CHAMPION

Have you ever considered that it should be her choice as to whether or not she should move her membership?

MS. BATES

I don't think she has a choice.

Another member, Robert Carr, breaks in –

ROBERT CARR

Pastor Champion, I apologize for my interruption, but I can't take anymore of this!

Member Carr reaches in his briefcase and takes out the By-Laws of the Church and holds it up and says –

ROBERT CARR (CONT'D)

Pastor Champion, I have reviewed our Church Constitution and By-Laws and nowhere in either does it say that a mother with a Black child cannot be a Member of this Church.

Another Member, Mildred Saxon, raises her hand and Dr. Champion acknowledges her -

DR. CHAMPION

Let us hear from Ms. Saxon.

MS. SAXON

Pastor Champion, some things are to be understood – you can't write everything in a Constitution or the By-Laws.

ROBERT CARR

Maybe so, Sister Saxon, but what's in the Constitution and By-Laws is the only thing that can be enforced.

The scene fast-forwards to the conclusion of the meeting and Dr. Champion is during a summary.

DR. CHAMPION

Folks, we have heard a number of "pros" and "cons" as regards to the asking Pat Smith to resign membership at St. Peter Baptist Church. I am fully aware that our Church Membership is

DR. CHAMPION (CONT'D)

> white and as your leader, I am guilty of not doing something to welcome any and all believers to join our fold. Pat has been a faithful member of our Church for more than twenty years – and I do mean a faithful member!

Pastor Champion pauses for a few moments, as stillness permeates the air, and he continues –

DR. CHAMPION (CONT'D)

> Jesus was our way shower, and he preached: "Whosoever will, let him come." Color on matters is our thinking! And, I for one, do not see where color has one thing to do with Christianity. As Pastor, I only have to vote in case of a tie. But, even though there was no tie, I want the record to show that I voted against asking Pat or any other member of this Church to resign membership based on such ungodly reasons! And for those of you who have said that you will resign membership of our fold if Pat does not, I wish you well and ask you to search your hearts and your conscious to see if your action represents the will of God! Amen!

The scene closes.

The scene opens and Patricia is at a neighborhood daycare to enroll J.J.

ATTENDANT

Good morning, Mrs. Smith. May I help you, please?

PATRICIA

Oh, yes! I am Patricia Smith, but I can see that you already know who I am.

ATTENDANT

Yes, mam, I have often seen you at St. Peters. I go there, too.

PATRICIA

I have a three-month old son that I would like to enroll here at "For Parents Who Care" Daycare.

The attendant pretends to be looking for the enrollment forms and apparently cannot find any. So, she remarks –

ATTENDANT

I must have run out of forms. Let me go and get some.

The attendant goes into the Office of the Manager, Mrs. Martha Ross, and informs her that Patricia is there to enroll her son.

ATTENDANT

Oh, my goodness, Mrs. Ross, Mrs. Patricia Smith is

Pointing to the outside of the office –

ATTENDANT (CONT'D)

Out there to enroll her three-month old son –

Attendant stretches her eyes and raises her arms and says –

ATTENDANT (CONT'D)

What on earth do I do?

MRS. ROSS

Just calm yourself, Patsy (attendant). Let me think!

A few minutes pass and Patricia sees a bell on the counter and proceeds to ring it. Mrs. Ross comes from her office and says –

MRS. ROSS

Mrs. Smith, I'm sorry but we are all filled-up!

PATRICIA

Then why is that sign out there that says – "Enroll your child today?"

MRS. ROSS

Oh, that sign, Patsy must have forgotten to take it down!

PATRICIA

Really! Well, I came here to enroll my baby, and the sign indicates that there are vacancies. So give me the forms.

MRS. ROSS

Mam, you are not in any position to call any shots at this Daycare!

In the midst of a heated dialogue, Mrs. Sarah Banks, the owner, walks in and greets Patricia –

MRS. BANKS

Hi, Pat! Is there a problem?

Mrs. Ross burst in –

MRS. ROSS

Yes, there is, Mrs. Banks! We told that woman that we have no vacancies and

Mrs. Banks interrupts and exclaims –

MRS. BANKS

Hold it, Martha! Hold it! We don't address customers as: That woman and you know better.

Mrs. Banks looks at Patricia and says –

MRS. BANKS (CONT'D)

Pat, I know what this is all about. But I am not operating a "color" Daycare! The only reason we don't have any Black babies is by parent's choice, not our Daycare choice!

Mrs. Banks turns to Martha and exclaims –

MRS. BANKS

Martha, I know that you were doing what you think I want you to do. But this Daycare is not going to discriminate against babies of a different color than white.

MARTHA

Well, ok, Mrs. Banks, but you know what this means!

MRS. BANKS

Yes, Martha, I know. But if parents want to take their babies somewhere else because of their prejudice and bigotry, then so beit!

The scene closes and opens three weeks later and Patricia is watching the Robinsville Evening News.

WXY-TV

Bulletin! Bulletin! Ladies and Gentlemen, this is WXY-TV Evening News and I am your Host, Mike Tyler. We were just informed that: "For

WXY-TV (CONT'D)

Parents Who Care" Daycare is expected to close within the next month, because of a Black baby, the son of Patricia Smith. The Owner, Mrs. Sarah Banks, said that 80% of her clients have stop bringing their babies to her Daycare. She is staying open until the parents who did not move their babies can find another facility for them.

The scene closes and opens and Patricia is watching the news.

PATRICIA

(Soliloquizing)

Oh, my God! Lord, what am I to do?

Patricia picks up J.J. and says to him –

\ ### PATRICIA

J.J., baby, all mama wants for you is what any mother wants for her child!

Holding J.J. in her arms and weeping, Patricia falls asleep and has a dream in which she is watching a trial in progress. The judge is making a ruling in a matter in which a wealthy man wants to short change a "bum" in wages. The Judge says –

JUDGE

Feller, you should be thankful to receive any wages. Millions of your kind wishes they could get a couple of dollars to buy a sandwich, rather than beg or steal!

BUM

Your Honor, Sir, yes, I am a bum. But does that deny me justice. I thought justice was a fixed thing, based on truth, rather than an idea on a scale that is to be moved up or down based on the persons' status under consideration.

The Judge pauses and thinks and responds –

JUDGE

Young man, of my twenty year as Judge, you have taught me the most valuable lesson I've ever learned. Indeed, Teddy Roosevelt said it best: "No man is justified in doing evil on the ground of expediency!"

The Judge looks at the wealthy business man and remarks –

JUDGE (CONT'D)

Sir, this Court finds you guilty of unfairly paying this man his due wages and order you to do so now, in the presence of the Court. Indeed, the test of a man is not in his running for cover with every threat of a storm. But in the courage he displays

JUDGE (CONT'D)

in navigating through the storm, safely to the other side where no refuge need be sought. Man must stand firm in the support of truth, even if he must stand alone. James Russell Lowell was correct: "Truth forever on the scaffold, wrong forever on the throne – yet that scaffold sways the future, and, behind that dim unknown, standeth God within the shadow, keeping watch above his own."

The Judge takes his gavel and raps three times and says –

JUDGE (CONT'D)

Case closed!

Patricia awakes from her dream and says to J.J.

PATRICIA

(Soliloquy)

J.J., I know now that mama is right and just. One day you'll be a man and you will have to make decisions for yourself. But, right now, mama has to do what is right!

The scene closes and depicts Dr. Champion deplaning at the airport in Atlanta, Georgia and bumps into John, J.J.'s father. They shake hands and Dr. Champion says –

DR. CHAMPION

John, I hope all is well with you!

John pauses for a few moments and responds –

JOHN

Pastor Champion, my life is a nightmare! I wish I could bring myself to believe that Pat was not unfaithful to me!

DR. CHAMPION

Well, all I can say is, if she is lying, she's better at it than anyone I have ever known.

JOHN

How are they – she and the boy?

DR. CHAMPION

John, does it bother you to refer to your son by name – J.J.?

JOHN

I wish I were as certain as you seem to be Pastor!

DR. CHAMPION

I don't think I follow you, John.

JOHN

You said, in referring to J.J., your Son! Has a nice ring to it, but how could that be.

It's silent for a moment, then John says –

JOHN (CONT'D)

After all, Pastor, do you think Joseph would have believed Mary had not an angel come from heaven and explained things to him?

Dr. Champion smiles and retorts –

DR. CHAMPION

You gotta point there – I wonder? I wonder?

JOHN

Pastor, you never did answer my question: How are they – Patricia and J.J.?

DR. CHAMPION

You said it – J.J.

Both John and Dr. Champion have a good old fashion Lol!

DR. CHAMPION

Well, John, Pat has had her "ups" and "downs!" And mostly, "downs!" I was born and raised in a segregated society, but I never knew that people could be so narrow-minded and blinded by color!

JOHN

Pastor Champion, it's normal, even among animals. Do you ever see sparrows and robins flying together or fish of different species swimming together?

It's silent for a few moments, then John says –

JOHN

No response, Pastor?

DR. CHAMPION

John, two points of significance you fail to consider. Point 1: Animals are created void of any ability to evaluate or make choices. It is by instinct that they form an association. Point 2: As for flying and swimming, the birds and fish are not limited as to where they fly or swim. If God is of no respecter of person, what makes you feel that we, created in His Image, should be?

JOHN

Well, Pastor, I guess I'm waiting for an answer.

DR. CHAMPION

Answer to what, my Boy? I don't know how you can possibly doubt Pat's faithfulness to you as a wife. If she were not, someone

DR. CHAMPION (CONT'D)

else would know it and some of those someone elses would have come forward and exposed her.

The scene closes as passengers for Dr. Champion's plane are asked to board. Dr. Champion and John shake hands and embrace. The scene opens and Pat is home with J.J., he is now six years old and ready for first grade.

J.J.

Mama, why are there twelve grades in school? Why not five or six?

PATRICIA

Well, J.J. think of all the land granddaddy Julian has. Why do you think he needs lots of days to plant the seeds we saw him planting?

J.J.

Oh, goodness, mama, that's too much to do in one day.

PATRICIA

Good, J.J. a child has so much to learn to grow up and get ready to go to college or to some, what we call trade school – too much to learn in five or six years. So people decide what they need to learn and let them learn a little each year for twelve years.

                    J.J.

That makes sense, mama. I like that so I won't have to try to learn too much in a hurry!

                  PATRICIA

Good Boy, J.J.

The scene closes and opens at Robinsville Elementary. Patricia is taking J.J. to school the first day. Dr. Marian Tyler, Principal, is waiting at the classroom and greets Patricia

                  DR. TYLER

Good morning, Mrs. Smith. I regret to inform you that Robinsville Elementary does not admit colored children.

                  PATRICIA

If something is colored, it has to be colored some color. My son is not colored any color, and

Pulling his acceptance papers from her bag, Patricia says –

              PATRICIA (CONT'D)

Principal Tyler, I have here in my hand my son's acceptance letter.

DR. TYLER

But that letter was sent on the assumption that your child was white!

Patricia shrugs her shoulders and exclaims –

PATRICIA

Then, since his mother and father are both white, I would assume that he is, too. And I expect him to be admitted to this school!

Principal Tyler had already called the Police and they arrive on the scene and accost Patricia.

CAPT. BOYD

Mrs. Smith, I am here to issue you an official order to vacate this property and take your child with you or I have no alternative but to place you under arrest.

PATRICIA

Then, do what you must, officer, because I am not leaving voluntarily!

The scene depicts Capt. Boyd putting cuffs on Patricia and taking her to his vehicle along with her son. The scene closes and opens at the Police Department; News Media are there to greet Patricia and J.J. as they are escorted from the car into the Police Department. Talking to Patricia –

WXY-TV

Mrs. Smith, what are your comments about this matter?

PATRICIA

It should not be what are my comments – it should be what's WXY-TV's comments and what is America's comments!

As they get inside of the station, Pat's father, Julian Foxx, has heard the news and is on hand –

WXY-TV

Mr. Foxx, what are your reactions to the arrest of your daughter and her son – your grandson?

MR. FOXX

This is outrageous, and this Police Department and this City will hear from me. My daughter was born and raised here, and the

MR. FOXX (CONT'D)

Foxx Enterprises pay more than fifty percent of the tax revenue to the City.

The Mayor, Pete Carter, comes out of his office and greets Mr. Foxx –

MAYOR CARTER

Mr. Foxx, Sir, the Police Officers were not acting on any orders from my office.

MR. FOXX

Mr. Mayor, it doesn't matter under whose orders Capt. Boyd acted, I am demanding an opened apology from this Department to my daughter and her little six-year old son – This is inexcusable!

MAYOR CARTER

Yes, Sir, Mr. Foxx, it shall be done!

The scene closes and J.J. is talking to his grandfather, Mr. Foxx –

J.J.

Granpa, what did mama and I do? Did we do anything wrong?

MR. FOXX

No, J.J. you and mama didn't do anything wrong!

J.J.

Then why did that policeman put those things on mama's hands? She must have done something wrong! She doesn't punish me, grandpa, unless I

J.J. (CONT'D)

have done something wrong!

Mr. Foxx picks J.J. up and says to him –

MR. FOXX

J.J. you are a little boy and sometimes people do things that a little boy can't understand –

J.J.

If mama didn't do anything wrong, grandpa, then that policeman was wrong – wasn't he, grandpa?

MR. FOXX

Yes, he was wrong, J.J.

The scene opens and Dr. Champion is ringing the doorbell at Patricia's home and she's answering it.

PATRICIA

Hello, Pastor Champion. Come in, it's good to see you.

DR. CHAMPION

Yes, what happened the other day at the school was terrible and I had to come and check on you and J.J.

PATRICIA

Come on in, Pastor and sit for a while.

Dr. Champion comes in and follows Patricia to the living room area and Patricia motions to him and says –

PATRICIA (CONT'D)

Sit down Pastor Champion

Pastor Champion sits down and remarks –

DR. CHAMPION

Well, how are you and J.J. doing, Pat? How did that police incident affect J.J.?

PATRICIA

As you know, J.J. is a very inquisitive kid. He tried to put two and two together and get four, but kept coming out with five! He has been taught that people should be good and do what's right and when people are being punished, so to speak, he wonders if they have done something wrong.

DR. CHAMPION

Yes, I can see, Pat. They ruffled Julian's (Pat's father) feathers and they surely do not want to do that – too much at stake!

PATRICIA

Pastor Champion, you know, nothing just happens; everything is caused and has a message for us.

DR. CHAMPION

I agree, Pat, but what message in this for us?

PATRICIA

Pastor Champion, I was raised in a segregated society. But lots of colored kids were my playmates. Surely, I knew that we had the inside track, but I never saw the true picture.

DR. CHAMPION

I'm not sure that I follow you, Pat.

PATRICIA

I guess what I am really trying to say is that the problem of racism in this country is rooted in the bigotry of our parents and grandparents, and its root is in economic and prestige. Mama didn't need a cook because she was unable to cook. If so, why did and do all wealthy whites hire black women to cook? To employ a white cook or butler would only display financial dominance. But to employ Negroes show racial dominance and that's what motivates the system.

DR. CHAMPION

Makes good sense to me. It's difficult to feel racially superior to people of your own color. Smarter, perhaps! Better, no!

PATRICIA

After this is over, I think I'm going to be a Civil Rights Advocate.

DR. CHAMPION

Yes, you will make a good one! What in this episode made you feel this way?

Patricia pauses for a few moments and remarks –

PATRICIA

You know, Pastor, I was raised in a racially segregated society. My parents had Negro helpers and I often played with their kids. But I guess I just assumed that was the way God wanted it to be and really saw nothing wrong with the status quo!

DR. CHAMPION

And now?

Patricia shrugs her shoulders and exclaims –

PATRICIA

There's old saying, Pastor, which meant little or nothing to me when I heard it: You can't tell me how I feel unless you have worn my moccasins!

DR. CHAMPION

Got a point, Pat. I guess I, too, always felt somewhat the way you feel.

PATRICIA

You know, Pastor Champion, an unknown made a profound statement that is a sermon that all America should hear weekly, if not, daily for a spell. Here it is: "We can all learn a lot from crayons. Some are pretty; some are sharp; some are dull; some are dark; some are light; some are bright; and some have weird names. But they all have learned to live together in the same box!"

DR. CHAMPION

Well said, my child. But on this high and good note, I must go.

PATRICIA

I understand, Pastor Champion, but thanks for your concern and for stopping by today to check on J.J. and me.

The scene closes as Patricia and Dr. Champion shake hands and embrace. The scene opens and J.J. is having child's talk with his mama –

J.J.

Mama, why don't the people at the school like me? Have I done anything wrong to them? Mama, I say my prayers at night. So am I a bad child?

PATRICIA

Oh, no, J.J. you haven't done anything to them! And, yes, you do say your prayers at night. So you are a good boy – mama's good little man!

J.J.

Then why don't they want me to go to school there, mama?

Patricia picks up J.J. and embraces him and the scene closes as she weeps with J.J. in her arms and says –

PATRICIA

It's ok honey! Mama will take care of you!

The scene opens and Patricia, Mr. Julian Foxx is visiting the Superintendant, Dr. Daniel Price.

DR. PRICE

Mr. Foxx, I can understand why you are upset!

MR. FOXX

The hell you can! Daniel, Pat has been an integral part of that community for almost twenty years.

MR. FOXX (CONT'D)

And now, because her child looks black, everybody now thinks of her as a misfit!

DR. PRICE

I don't think that's accurate, Mr. Foxx. It's just

Mr. Foxx breaks in –

MR. FOXX

It's just what? It is as simple as one plus one is two, those bigots don't want my grandson to attend that damn school! And I will take this matter all the way to the Supreme Court, if I have to!

DR. PRICE

But what can I do? My hands are tied!

MR. FOXX

Like hell, they are tied! Let me ask you a question and I want a damn simple answer - Do you think Pat has the right to put her child in that school?

DR. PRICE

Well, Mr. Foxx

Mr. Foxx, cuts in and retorts –

MR. FOXX

No wells! Just give me a damn simple answer – yes or no!!!

DR. PRICE

Pat has the right, Sir, but her rights conflict with the Law!

MR. FOXX

So! Then, when the Law and one's God given rights conflict, what should you do? Yes, what should you do?

DR. PRICE

I think we should try to change the Law, but it takes time to change a Law that has been a custom for centuries.

MR. FOXX

By that time, J.J. will be fighting to get his child in the school!

DR. PRICE

Sir, I know deep down in my soul that it's wrong to deny J.J. or any other child the right to attend that school or any other school, but what am I to do?

Mr. Foxx stands and says –

MR. FOXX

Superintendent Price, I don't think your hands are tied – your conscience is tied by fear – fear of what the consequence of the election next year, at which time, your term expires.

Mr. Foxx, gets up from his chair, looks Dr. Price in the eyes and exclaims –

MR. FOXX (CONT'D)

John Burke is still right, Mr. Superintendent: "All is necessary for evil to triumph is for good men to do nothing."

The scene closes. Patricia has filed a lawsuit in the District Court against the Public School System in Robinsville. In the meantime, she has hired the best to teach J.J. at home. The scene opens at the first Court hearing of the case. Judge Gregory Carter is presiding and is making his introductory remarks –

JUDGE CARTER

Ladies and Gentlemen, the Court convenes to hear the case: Patricia Smith vs The Board of Education, State of East Virginia. The Court is ready to hear opening statements.

Judge Carter looks at Attorney Mack Duffie and says –

JUDGE CARTER (CONT'D)

Is the accuse ready?

ATTY. DUFFIE

Yes, your Honor, the Accuse is ready.

Judge Carter looks to Attorney Ben Tate and says –

JUDGE CARTER

Is the Defense ready?

ATTY. CARTER

Yes, Your Honor, The Defense is ready.

JUDGE CARTER

You may proceed, Attorney Duffie.

Attorney Duffie walks before the Jury and says –

ATTY. DUFFIE

Members of the Jury, I represent Mrs. Patricia Smith who has filed charges against The Board of Education, State of East Virginia. Mrs. Smith is a resident of Robinsville, East

ATTY. DUFFIE (CONT'D)

Virginia. She was born and raised there and lived in her neighborhood for the past twenty years. She has a son who has been refused enrollment privileges in Robinsville Elementary School because of the color of his skin (Black). The Accuse will show that such action violates that

ATTY. DUFFIE (CONT'D)

child's Civil Rights on the basis of his mother and father.

The scene fast-forwards to the concluding statements of the Attorney of the Defense.

ATTY. TATE

Ladies and Gentlemen of the Jury. The Defense will show that based on the Laws of the Sovereign State of East Virginia, Robinsville Elementary has every right to deny J.J. Smith admission.

The scene fast-forwards to the Judge's responses to the introductory statements by the Accuse and the Defense.

JUDGE CARTER

Members of the Jury, you have heard introductory statements by both the Accuse and the Defense. The Court charges each of you to hear the arguments of both and render a verdict of guilty or not guilty base on the evidence presented.

The scene depicts Patricia taking the Oath of Obligation as a witness.

JUDGE

Please be seated.

ATTY. TATE

Mrs. Smith, please tell the Court why your son, J.J. was denied admission to Robinsville Elementary School in Robinsville, VA.

PATRICIA

My son, J.J. is being denied because of the color of his skin.

ATTY. TATE

Mrs. Smith, please be more specific. When you say based on the color of his skin, what color do you refer? White? Brown, Yellow?

PATRICIA

Black.

ATTY. TATE

Then, you are saying that your son is black!

Attorney Duffie, says –

ATTY. DUFFIE

Your Honor, I object. Perhaps, Atty. Tate needs to define what it means to be Black.

JUDGE CARTER

Objection over-ruled. The witness will answer the question.

PATRICIA

No, my son is not Black, he is White!

ATTY. TATE

Mrs. Smith, is your son's color the some complexion as yours?

PATRICIA

No, it's not!

ATTY. TATE

Is the skin color of your son the same as that of persons called Negroes or Colored?

PATRICIA

Yes!

ATTY. TATE

Then, based on the criteria of observation, it is covert to say that your child is a Negro or a Colored boy?

PATRICIA

I am white and my son's father is white. Therefore, our son is white.

Atty. Tate pauses for a moment – and softly says –

ATTY. TATE

Is it not a fact that your husband divorced you on the assumption that your son is a Negro boy?

PATRICIA

Yes!

ATTY. TATE

No further questions, Your Honor.

Atty. Duffie walks to the witness position and says softly —

ATTY. DUFFIE

Mrs. Smith, is it not true that your husband paid some of the best private detectives in the nation to investigate to see if there could be found any evidence to support his claim that you had an affair with a Negro and got pregnant and had his (The Negroes) baby?

PATRICIA

Yes, that is true!

The scene fast-forwards to closing statements.

ATTY. TATE

Ladies and Gentlemen of the Jury, it has been established that Mrs. Smith's son, J.J. is a Negro! The test of one's being a Negro or white is based

ATTY. TATE (CONT'D)

on the color of that person's skin. And Mrs. Smith's son's skin color is Black. Therefore, we have to assume that he is Black. The Laws of the Sovereign State of East Virginia prohibits the enrollment of Black and white children at the same school. Therefore, the Defense rules that the Board of Education of the Sovereign State of East Virginia is justified in denying Mrs. Smith's son admission to Robinsville Elementary School.

ATTY. DUFFIE

Ladies and Gentlemen of the Jury, the Defense has presented a cogent argument that Mrs. Smith's son, J.J., should not be granted, legally, admission to Robinsville Elementary School. The Accused has never denied that her son's skin is Black. However, three DNA Analyses were done to ascertain if the child's father is white and each analysis confirm that he is. Moreover, Mr. Smith, Mrs. Smith's ex-husband, employed the best private detectives in the business to prove the contrary and not a shred of evidence was found to deny this fact. Indeed, mutations are rare, but they do happen. For years, it was believed that all swans were white. But that assumption was proven false. I submit to you, Members of the Jury, that this is a case of a mutation. Thus, despite the boy's color, both his mother and father are white and so is he biologically, and should be

ATTY. DUFFIE (CONT'D)

granted admission to Robinsville Elementary School, Robinsville, East Virginia.

JUDGE CARTER

Members of the Jury, you have heard very cogent arguments from both the Accuse and the Defense. Indeed, your task is not an easy one. Nevertheless, you are charged to weigh the evidence presented to you and bring back a verdict of guilty or not guilty. Because of the nature of this Case, the Court will delay the verdict. Today is Friday, May 14, 1954. We will reconvene Court on Wednesday, May, 19, 1954. At that time we will expect a verdict. As usual, you are not to discuss this Case with anyone other than a juror.

Judge Carter sounds the gavel and says –

JUDGE CARTER (CONT'D)

Court Recesses!

However, on Monday, May 17, 1954, Chief Justice Earl Warren of the Supreme Court of the United States announces that, in the Case of: Brown vs Board of Education, Topeka, Kansas, the Court ruled unanimously that segregation of Public School on the basis of Separate but Equal is Unconstitutional.

The scene opens and Court is in session on May 19, 1954. Judge Carter, presiding.

JUDGE CARTER

Ladies and Gentlemen and Members of the Jury. The Court convenes to hear the verdict of Patricia Smith vs The Board of Education of the State of East VA. As you no doubt know that the Supreme Court has ruled that segregation in our Public Schools on the basis of "Separate but Equal" is Unconstitutional. The Court will entertain the verdict and make its ruling.

Judge Carter looks to the Jury and asks –

JUDGE CARTER (CONT'D)

Has the Jury reached a verdict?

MEMBERS OF THE JURY

Yes, Your Honor!

A Member of the Jury hands the decision to the Clerk and she passes it to the Judge. He reads it and exclaims –

JUDGE CARTER

The Members of the Jury found The Board of Education of Sovereign State of East Virginia: Not Guilty. The Court thanks the Members of the Jury for its work in hearing the Case and reaching a Verdict.

Many members of the audience are cheering and applauding the Verdict of Not Guilty. After a brief period of applauding, the Judge raps his gavel and says –

JUDGE CARTER

Ladies and Gentlemen, notwithstanding the ruling of the Jury, the Highest Court in the Land has rule against the Separation of Schools. It is now the Law of this nation to prohibit the segregation of schools by Law. And this Court will not rule in opposition to the Supreme Court's Ruling. Therefore, this Court hereby disallows the Verdict of Not Guilty in the Case: Patricia Smith vs The Board of Education of East Virginia and rules that the Son of Mrs. Patricia Smith cannot be denied admission to Robinsville Elementary School based on race.

Some members of the Court render boos and others applaud. Judge Carter raps his gavel and says –

JUDGE CARTER

Order in the Court! Ladies and Gentlemen, we are not required to agree with the Law, but we are required to obey the Law. That is the virtue and spirit of Democracy! As long as Segregation of our public schools was within in Law, This Court upheld that Law. Now that Law has been ruled by the United States Supreme Court as Unconstitutional, this Court shall uphold this new

JUDGE CARTER (CONT'D)

Law. This is what is expected and required of every citizen.

Things settle to normality and the scene ends as Judge Carter, sounds the gavel and says –

JUDGE CARTER (CONT'D)

The Court adjourns!

News Reporters are taking pictures and asking Patricia questions –

REPORTER #1

Mrs. Smith, how do you feel about the ruling?

Wiping tears, Patricia says –

PATRICIA

Naturally, I am pleased and gratified. But I am also saddened!

REPORTER #1

Why are you saddened? You got what you wanted and tried so hard to get! Why are you saddened by the results?

PATRICIA

It's bad when nine persons have to dictate to so many what's just!

Looking across the audience, Patricia wipes tears and says –

PATRICIA (CONT'D)

There isn't one – no, not one person against this Court ruling would want his or her child denied the rights that my son was denied! What happened to the "Golden Rule?"

REPORTER #2

Mrs. Smith, did you ever consider sending your son to a school attended only by Negroes? If not, why not?

PATRICIA

No! Absolutely not!

REPORTER #2

Could it have been that you thought your son to be better than the Negro kids?

PATRICIA

No! I never considered sending my son to an all Negro school, because to have done so would not have indicated that I thought him to be more than Negro kids, but less than white kids!

REPORTER #1

Mrs. Smith, you grew up in a home where your parents had maids and servants. Did you ever think you were more than they were?

It's silent for a few moments, then Patricia responds –

PATRICIA

I am certain that, watching Negro men much older than my father come to my daddy and say yes sir to him, call him mister and he called them by their first name, I was indoctrinated to believe that I was. So the answer to your question is, yes!

REPORTER #2

How do you feel about it now?

PATRICIA

This experience has taught me "first-hand" that: "As you have done it to the least of these my brethren, you have done it unto me." Prior to this experience much of what I heard about brotherly love was just talk!

REPORTER #2

Then who is the blame, in your opinion, for whites to feel that they are better than Negroes?

PATRICIA

Those who teach them to hate!

REPORTER #1

Do you think that there are whites who are telling their kids to hate Negroes?

PATRICIA

Yes! Indeed!

REPORTER #1

I'm not sure I follow you. Are you saying that there are whites who really tell their kids: "Hate Negroes?"

PATRICIA

There are lots of ways to teach: What we say; how we act; etc. Children learn what they live, Sir. And unless they live hate, they won't hate!

The scene fast-forwards to the conclusion of the reporter's and Patricia's dialogue –

REPORTER #1

Mrs. Smith, we thank you for your forthright responses to our questions. And I am certain that they have given us a lot to think about. Let us hope that all of us can learn vicariously from yours and similar experiences and begin to take seriously bringing about the Fatherhood of God and the Brotherhood of Man, which is the path-

REPORTER #1 (CONT'D)

way to peace on earth and goodwill among men!

The scene closes and opens at Macedonia Baptist Church in Clarksdale, East Virginia. The Pastor, Dr. Ralph Webbs, has called the meeting at the request of Mr. Julian Foxx, Patricia Smith's Father. Clarksdale is the largest rural area in Clarksdale and Mr. Foxx owns more than seventy percent of the property and produces more than eighty percent of all the tobacco and corn in the area. Dr. Webbs is speaking –

DR. WEBBS

Gentlemen, I called this meeting at the request of our former Chairman of our Deacon Board. He has a concern that he wishes to discuss with this Board. Let's hear him.

Those present applaud as Mr. Foxx stands; he looks at the ceiling for a few seconds and begins to say –

MR. FOXX

Gentlemen, let me thank our Pastor for convening this meeting and you for coming. During this summer, our grandson, J.J. came and stayed two weeks with his grandmama and granddaddy. Til and I go to Church every Sunday and, naturally, our grandson went with us.

Mr. Foxx shrugs his shoulders and says –

MR. FOXX (CONT'D)

Nobody said anything, that is with their tongues. But lots of people speak very loudly and clearly with their actions – strong looks! No looks!

Mr. Foxx smiles and chuckles and says –

MR. FOXX (CONT'D)

Was I shocked by this strange behavior? Not at all! As a matter of fact when Pat brought J.J. home, at first I behaved quite irrationally, as any southern-raised father would behave.

Mr. Foxx raises his right hand and bangs the ball of it on a nearby table and exclaims –

MR. FOXX (CONT'D)

But my behavior was not because I felt in any way that my daughter had an affair with a Negro! It was custom! Yes, a custom to which I had been exposed to for more than half a century.

It is very still – everyone is listening to Mr. Foxx with great intensity. Mr. Foxx continues –

MR. FOXX

You know, I'm not nearly smart enough to fathom the ways of God. But I do know that He has always spoken to us in varied ways, and I believe that He is speaking to us through this incident of

MR. FOXX (CONT'D)

my child – a white woman – brought forth a Negro looking child!

Deacon Melvin Green raised his hand and Mr. Foxx sees him and says –

MR. FOXX (CONT'D)

Ok, Mel.

MELVIN

Mr. Foxx, what do you feel God is saying in this situation? And why to us?

Mr. Foxx smiles and says –

MR. FOXX

Mel, I asked myself that same question, seemingly million times and it came to me. As some of you know, my daddy, Senior Foxx, was probably one of the most segregated thinking white man in all of Allen County! We were indoctrinated by words and actions to believe that whites are better and superior to Negroes! And we have perpetuated that false belief.

MEL

If we are not better and superior, then why is it that we are their bosses and, for the most part, determine their destinies?

Mr. Foxx pauses for a few seconds and remarks –

MR. FOXX

Mel, if we are indeed superior, how do you count for Jack Johnson and Joe Louis becoming Heavyweight Champions by beating the superior white man.

MEL

Mr. Foxx, an ox can pull far more weight than any man! Does that mean the ox is superior or on equal par with man? I don't think so. It's simple a measure of strength – that's all!

MR. FOXX

Well taken, Bro. Mel. Then answer this for me: If whites are superior to Negroes why wasn't Booker T. Washington, the man who saved the South with his ingenuity of the peanut, white? The same can be said of Garrett Morgan and the men who invented: The elevator, the lawn mower, the ballpoint pen, the comb, dust pan and countless other inventions that we enjoy.

MEL

That's something to think about. But how does this tie in to the matter at hand?

MR. FOXX

Those of us here in this room constitute the power in Allen County for weal or woe. People look to us for leadership and advice. I think this incident is an opportunity to bring about harmony, peace and goodwill among whites and Negroes.

MEL

And how on God's green earth do we do that, Mr. Foxx?

MR. FOXX

We can begin right now by, for ten seconds, put on and wear the moccasins of the Negro. Yes, ask yourself is the way we treat those who share crop for us Godly?

Looking at Dr. Webbs, Mr. Foxx exclaims –

MR. FOXX (CONT'D)

Let's here from our Pastor. Let him put the conclusion in perspective!

DR. WEBBS

Well, Gents, I admit that I had not given this matter the consideration it's due. If peace on earth and goodwill among men is to ever exists, it seems as if the Church should be its origins. I think the problem is basically fright of dating within the races.

It's quiet for a few moments, then Dr. Webbs says –

> DR. WEBBS
>
> I paused to give you a moment of sigh! Indeed, that has always been the conceived problem. And the person who thinks that way and feels that a white woman is too pure and too good to date a Negro should feel that the likelihood of such is impossible! Indeed, dating across color-lines would occur far less than most of you think! Let us begin by inviting all races to attend our Church functions and treat men like men and women like women regardless of race. What we do will set the example for others to follow. This has been a rewarding and worthwhile meeting and will hopefully be the beginning of a step toward the advent of the Fatherhood of God and the Brotherhood of man.

The scene closes and opens at Robinsville Elementary Pre-planning. Principal Dr. Marian Tyler is talking –

> DR. TYLER
>
> Welcome back, Teachers. Hope each of you had a very restful summer and we are back and ready to hit "the saddle" again. We have a number of items on our agenda. But the most pressing and

DR. TYLER (CONT'D)

urgent one is to put to rest what anyone might think about our admitting two Negro students this year.

A teacher, Bettye Rich, raises her hand and Dr. Tyler recognizes her and remarks –

DR. TYLER

Ok, Ms. Rich, your concern, please.

MS. RICH

Just how are we to treat them?

DR. TYLER

By them, I assume the two Negro students.

MS. RICH

Yes, that is correct!

DR. TYLER

That's simple, Bettye – Just treat them the way you treat any student.

MS. RICH

I grossly oppose letting them attend Robinsville! Then, how can you expect me to act like I want them here?

DR. TYLER

Bettye, The Highest Court in the Land ruled that we cannot deny these students admission based on their color!

MS. RICH

Those nine persons who made that decision have no right to enforce their thinking on us.

DR. TYLER

Bettye, those persons are appointed to their positions by the President of the United States and approved by the Senate. Thus, we are duly obligated to accept these two students and to treat them as we do all others.

MS. RICH

I don't think I can do that! In fact, I know I can't!

It's silent for a few moments and Dr. Tyler responds –

DR. TYLER

You have made it clear what your opinions are and of your actions in this regard. Therefore, I am asking you to resign your position here at Robinsville Elementary, effective today! There will be no violation of this Court order at this school.

Dr. Tyler looks around the room and exclaims –

DR. TYLER (CONT'D)

Are there any further comments on this matter or are there other person or persons who share Bettye's opinion? If so, speak now and, if not, I expect all Teachers here at Robinsville to act in accordance to this Court Mandate!

The scene fast-forwards to the conclusion of the meeting and Roy Mays is talking –

ROY MAYS

Principal Tyler. I appreciate your position on this matter. It is past time for those of us, and I mean everybody in this nation to begin to see all human being as they are – human beings. I would like to ask Bettye or anyone else to give me one sensible reason Negro kids should be prohibited from attending our school!

DR. TYLER

Thanks Roy for those pertinent remarks. America is the Country of all its citizens, not just those who are called white!

Looking at the faculty, Dr. Tyler concludes –

DR. TYLER (CONT'D)

Let us conclude this meeting – in a spirit of goodwill and with a sense of dedication and commitment that will make this year and every year, a "Banner Year."

The scene closes and opens at Patricia's home, and she and J.J. are in conversation.

J.J.

Mama, why do you call Patsy (The Maid) Patsy and she calls you Mrs. Smith? She older than you, isn't she? And I call her Patsy, but Marc calls you Mrs. Foxx, too.

Patricia is silent for a moment and says –

PATRICIA

You know, J.J. I never told her to call me Mrs. Smith. But now that you have made me think of it, I will change that!

Patsy and Marc walk in and speak –

PATSY

Hi, Mrs. Foxx, you and J.J.

J.J. looks at Patricia and she says –

PATRICIA

Patsy, you and Marc come in here for a moment, please.

Patsy takes Marc by the hand and they come in the room where Patricia and J.J. are –

PATSY

Ok, Mrs. Pat, what is the verdict.

Patricia smiles and says –

PATRICIA

What's your birthdate?

PATSY

Oh, Mrs. Smith, a lady is never to reveal her age!

They both have a good old fashion Lol and Patricia says –

PATRICIA

I was just wondering who is the older – you or I?

PATSY

I think I got you by three months and five days.

PATRICIA

Then neither of us is old enough to be called "Mrs." by the other! So starting right now, you will address me as Pat and I you as Patsy – ok?

Patsy shrugs her shoulders and says –

PATSY

Ok by me – Pat!

Then Patricia, looking at J.J. and Marc says, pointing at Patsy and herself –

PATRICIA

For you, two: For you J.J. she is Ms. Patsy and for you Marc, I'm Ms. Pat.

Both boys laugh and gives an acceptable gesture.

The scene closes and opens and Patricia gets from her mailbox a letter from Robinsville Elementary informing her that J.J.'s admission has been approved. Patricia has decided to send J.J. to Excelsior Elementary for Negroes. She is in dialogue with Dr. Champion.

DR. CHAMPION

Pat, I cannot understand you're not wanting to send J.J. to that school. This was your desire and you went to Court and fought for that right!

PATRICIA

Yes, you are right, Pastor! But I fought because I felt that my rights were not being honored. I was not trying to enroll J.J. at Robinsville Elementary because I thought it was better than the Negro Schools, but because the kids at Robinsville Elementary are not better than J.J.

DR. CHAMPION

I agree wholeheartedly, Pat.

The scene closes and opens at John's Enterprise in Burbank, California. John is sitting looking at a picture of Patricia on his desk and a co-worker, Randy Patterson, comes by his room, sees him and knocks and John responds –

JOHN

Oh, come in Randy.

Randy walks in takes a seat and says to John –

RANDY

John, quite often, I see you sitting there staring at her picture; you'll never forget her with her picture always before you.

John looks at Randy and says –

JOHN

You are right, Randy. But I am not sure that I want to forget her nor can I ever forget her.

RANDY

Maybe you should think about making amends!

JOHN

More than a million times, I have entertained that thought.

RANDY

And, so?

JOHN

I am in a maelstrom, a quagmire of confusion – you name it!

John looks directly at Randy and remarks –

JOHN (CONT'D)

Man, I honestly believe that Pat was a gift from God! She was everything I could have ever hoped for!

RANDY

Then, if she was a gift from God, why would He (God) let this happen?

JOHN

Randy, my Boy, that's the "Sixty-Four Thousand Dollar" question. I firmly believe that every encounter we have contains a lesson for our spiritual and mental growth. But, I just can't seem to determine what that lesson is in this case.

RANDY

Have you called her just to say hello and ask how she and your son or the boy is doing?

JOHN

God knows I have wanted to call and do that, but I just couldn't bring myself to do it. My world had eclipsed!

                           RANDY

And the longer you put it off the less you will want to and the more difficult it will be to do so.

                           JOHN

The latter part of your statement is true, but not the former –

                           RANDY

Don't follow you, John.

                           JOHN

Put it off does not, in anyway, diminish my desire to call Pat. But it becomes more difficult, because I try to find more and more reasons not to do so.

Randy stands and says –

                           RANDY

Well, Oh Buddy, I had better get back to the "grinding stone." I've got a "deadline" on that LST Project and I'm a bit off schedule.

                           JOHN

You'll make it –

The scene closes as Randy pats John on the back and says –

RANDY

It will eventually resolve itself.

The scene opens and John is talking to his Office Manager, Ruby King.

JOHN

Ruby, call around town at every University and find out who is the most profound and noteworthy geneticist in town.

RUBY

Ok, right away, Mr. Smith.

Ruby is about to exit John's Office and he says –

JOHN

Oh, Ruby, let me know as soon as you find something, even if I'm in an executive meeting!

RUBY

Will do, Mr. Smith.

The scene closes and opens at Mr. and Mrs. Foxx's (Patricia's parents) home –

MRS. FOXX

Jul (Julian) how did the meeting go at the called meeting of the Deacon Board the other night? You never mentioned it to me.

MR. FOXX

Til (Matilda), it went fine. Naturally, there were some skeptics, but I think everyone, including me, got a darn good look at the man in the mirror and neither of us was pleased with what we saw.

MRS. FOXX

It's hard to believe that we believe that all of us, Negroes and whites, are God's children. God is of no respecter person, and yet, we feel that He made some of us superior to others.

MR. FOXX

I really, deep within, don't believe anyone believes that. It just has been convenient to act that way.

MRS. FOXX

Too, no one dared ever question his own motive about the race issue. It just seems better to believe or at least accept what is materially in your best interest.

MR. FOXX

America is the greatest country in the world and has always been a model for other countries. Thus, we should set an example for the rest of the world to let the world see democracy exercised in our land, everywhere, and let our government

MR. FOXX (CONT"D)

really be a government of the people, for the people and by the people!

MRS. FOXX

Amen, Jul! Amen!

The scene closes and opens and John's Office Manager, Ruby King, is in his office talking with him –

RUBY

Mr. Smith, I checked every source and Dr. Moto Yen seems to be one of the world's best geneticists. And I made you an appointment with him for tomorrow at 10 A.M. I checked your schedule and you don't have anything scheduled until 2 P.M.

John jumps up and clasps his hand and exclaims –

JOHN

Good Girl, Ruby! Just call and confirm that I will be at his office for the 10 A.M. appointment.

The scene closes and opens and the next day at 9:45 A.M. and John is at the Office of Dr. Moto Yen.

SECRETARY

Good morning, Mr. Smith. Dr. Yen is expecting you and I will let him know that you are here.

JOHN

Thanks!

The Secretary rings and Dr. Yen answers –

DR. YEN

Yes, Mildred –

MILDRED

Dr. Yen, Mr. John Smith is here for his 10 A.M. appointment with you.

DR. YEN

Thanks, Mildred, admit him.

Mildred turns to John and says –

MILDRED

Mr. Smith, Dr. Yen will see you now.

Mildred escorts John to Dr. Yen's Office and knocks –

DR. YEN

Come in, Mildred!

Mildred opens the door and she and John walk in and she says –

MILDRED

Dr. Yen, This is Mr. John Smith, CEO and Owner of Smith's Enterprises.

Dr. Yen rises, shakes hands with John and motions for him to be seated.

DR. YEN

Being a CEO in your firm, what is your intense interest in genetics, Mr. Smith?

JOHN

It's a long story, Dr. Yen! I was married for fifteen years to a woman that was tailor-made for my euphoria.

DR. YEN

You said, was married – what could have happened to a tailor-made marriage?

The scene fast-forwards to the conclusion of John's explanation to Dr. Yen about the birth of J.J.

JOHN

So, Dr., it was too much for me to accept.

DR. YEN

I can understand your initial reaction, Mr. Smith, but once you had time to think thing through and the confidence you had in your wife, I can't see why you refused to believe her.

It's silent for a few moments, then Dr. Yen says –

DR. YEN

So, I surmise that you want my opinion as regards this mutation.

JOHN

Yes, Dr., that's about sizes it up!

DR. YEN

Mutation is an unexpected change in the species that cannot be explained by heredity. Rare, yes! Possible, yes!

Dr. Yen rubs his left hand across his face and says –

DR. YEN (CONT'D)

Strangely as it might seem, Mr. Smith, it is possible that a woman can become pregnant without a man and give birth. Genetics supports this claim, though I do not know of one instance that it happened.

JOHN

Maybe, just maybe, Pat was on the level.

DR. YEN

Mr. Smith, I have not had much training in the area of psychiatry, but I am willing to bet my "bottom dollar" that you can take out the 'maybe'

DR. YEN (CONT'D)

in your statement and say: "Pat was on the level."

JOHN

Are you saying that I am foxing, Dr?

DR. YEN

No, not at all. If so, you would know it, and it would not serve the purpose intended.

JOHN

Can't follow you, Dr. Yen!

DR. YEN

You see, Mr. Smith, in order for your claim to have any merit, you have to believe what you claim to be true.

JOHN

I see!

DR. YEN

And from what you told me about Pat, I feel absolutely assured that your son was an example of a mutation!

The scene fast-forwards to the conclusion of Johns and Dr. Yen's meeting –

JOHN

I thank you, Dr. Yen. And I shall pray over this matter and make a decision soon.

DR. YEN

Good luck, my Son and be blessed!

The scene closes and opens and Patricia is at home discussing her decision to enroll J.J. in a presently all Negro School –

MR. FOXX

Pat, I can understand your points of view, but since J.J. skin is Black, I feel that it would be better to enroll him at Robinsville Elementary.

MRS. FOXX

Yes, Jul and that fits in what we are trying to accomplish.

PATRICIA

I don't understand, mama.

MR. FOXX

Some of us leading citizens here in Allen County met to discuss the unfair, fair and most of all, unbiblical manner we have acted with Negroes. It was the consensus of all members of our Deacon Board to begin to promote peace, harmony and goodwill among the races.

MRS. FOXX

Pat, have you ever talked to J.J. about the difference in yours and his colors?

PAT

No, I haven't, mama.

MRS. FOXX

That's not good enough, Pat! Could it be that you really don't want him to know that he is conceived to be a Negro and you are white?

It's silent for a few moments and Mr. Foxx speaks out –

MR. FOXX

You see, Pat, right now, he is unaware that emphasis is placed on color and white is considered superior and Black inferior. It is better that you find a way to tell him than for someone in school to tell him.

MRS. FOXX

Right, Jul! Because the manner that someone else tells him might not be so pleasant.

PAT

That has crossed my mind numerous times. And you are right, the both of you! And I had better get with that and soon

                    MRS. FOXX

And the sooner, the better!

The scene closes and opens at a reception the CEOs are having at John's Office and the "Palatia Suite." John is sitting alone, looking in the Fountain, and a very attractive Blond, Bettye Rice, walks over and tosses three coins in the fountain and says –

                    BETTYE

Three coins in the Fountain, each one seeking happiness; thrown by three hopeful lovers, which one will the Fountain bless? Make it mine! Make it mine! Make it mine!

John looks at her and says –

                    JOHN

Three coins, a hundred and three coins, what difference will it make?

                    BETTYE

The difference is not in the number of coins, but in the ones who toss them.

                    JOHN

Metaphysically, Fountain is symbolic to one's heart and the three coins are symbolic to his thoughts and wishing is symbolic to nature of his thoughts.

                    BETTYE

Good analogy, but how will the Fountain answer the three hopeful lovers?

                    JOHN

Depends on the intensity of each person's hopes and expectations.

John turns to Bettye, looks at his watch and remarks –

                    JOHN

Well, the night is far spent and I had better go and get myself some "shut-eye."

                    BETTYE

It's never late, John, until 2 A.M. and that's early in the morning!

Bettye pats John on the left shoulder and says –

                    BETYE (CONT'D)

Remember, John: "All work and no play make John a dull boy!

                    JOHN

Maybe, Bettye. But dullness is in the mind of the beholder!

John and Bettye both smile and John gives her a faint wave of goodbye and the scene closes and opens and John is in bed. He is lying there pleasantly reminiscencing and he falls asleep and has a dream of the party that he and Pat had, celebrating the coming of their son. They are sitting watching everyone enjoying the party.

JOHN

Pat, this is the "Crowning Experience" of my being. How blessed!

PAT

Indeed, my love! We have waited so long – so very long for this moment! For whatever reason, only God, in His infinite wisdom, why so long!

JOHN

But it is true, Pat, that: "Nothing is long which comes to an end." Maybe there was a lesson in that waiting.

PAT

Maybe so, Dear! Maybe So! But it really doesn't matter now, we are going to have our baby boy and have a "forever" in our own way to live eternally together!

JOHN

And we will form a "trinity" that will bind our hearts, being inseparable even unto death!

Pat reaches over and their hands join and tears of joy run down her cheeks – John wakes and sits straight up in bed and exclaims –

JOHN

(Soliloquy)

Lord, what does this dream mean? What am I to do? I wonder how Pat and our son are doing? I need them, and I wonder if they need me? J.J. does not know me and I wonder if Pat ever tells him about me?

The scene closes and John is at the Airport in La getting ready to aboard the plane to Robinsville East Virginia. The scene depicts John boarding the plane and it's in the air. The scene fast-forwards and John is in a rental car driving to Pat's. He arrives and goes and rings the bell but nobody answers. He stands there and it dawns on him to try his key to the door. He tries it and it unlocks. But as he starts to walk in, he stops and locks the door and goes and sits in his car and pulls it over on the other side of the street and down the street about fifty yards from the house. Shortly, Pat and J.J. arrive.

Pat says to J.J., who is asleep in the car –

PAT

Wake up J.J. we are home!

J.J.

Ok, mama! Ok!

They get out of the car and walk to the door and as Pat begins to insert the key, she has a funny feeling that John has been there. She pauses and J.J. says –

                           J.J.

What is it mama? Why are you standing there like that?

                           PAT

J.J. I had what we grown-ups call a premonition – Don't worry about what it is!

                           J.J.

Ok, mama.

John watches from his car and just as he is about to leave, Patricia and J.J. come out of the house to take their dog, Rex, for a walk. She and J.J. are talking, laughing and having fun –

                         PATRICIA

J.J. I'll be happy when you can take Rex for a walk without me.

                           J.J.

Why, mama?

PATRICIA

I have things in the house I could be doing – like getting our supper ready.

J.J.

Mama, I thought that was Ms. Patsy's job.

PATRICIA

Yes, it is J.J, but I gave her today off. So, it's mama's job today.

John is still watching and thinking out loud –

JOHN

(Soliloquy)

Gee, how I wish all three of us could be walking the dog together. I should get out of this car and greet them.

Several cars are passing and John says –

JOHN

(Soliloquy)

As soon as these cars pass, I'm getting out – what will be, will be!

Finally, the traffic clears, but John's enthusiasm has waned and he thinks –

JOHN (CONT'D)

(Soliloquy)

Maybe this is not a good time. I'll come back another time when it's more suitable!

The scene fades and depicts John speeding away. Patricia and J.J. hear tires squeaking and turn and look and Patricia says to J.J. –

PATRICIA

J.J. that somebody must be in a big hurry to go!

The scene closes and opens as Patricia is about to do some oral experiment with J.J. She shows him a picture of a Black cat and a white mouse and says to him –

PATRICIA

J.J., which do you think is the superior of these two animals: The black cat or the white mouse?

J.J.

The black cat can beat the white mouse, mama.

PATRICIA

Right you are, J.J.

Then Patricia takes a picture of a black cat and a white stallion and says to JJ –

PATRICIA (CONT'D)

Now, J.J., which do you think is stronger and superior – the black cat or the white stallion?

J.J.

Mama, the white stallion is bigger and much stronger!

Then Patricia shows a picture of a white puppy and a black puppy and says –

PATRICIA

Now, J.J., which puppy do you think is the biggest, badest and most powerful of these two puppies?

J.J.

Mama, I can't tell!

PATRICIA

Why can't you tell, J.J.?

J.J.

Mama, I don't know what either one can or cannot do.

PATRICIA

Suppose I give them to two boys and the boy with the black puppy trains it do tricks and to hunt, but the other boy just keeps his puppy in his house

PATRICIA (CONT'D)

and feeds it and plays with it. Which puppy do you think will be more valuable to a man who owns a zoo?

J.J.

The black puppy, mama.

PATRICIA

Suppose we switch and the boy who trains his puppy to do tricks and hunt just lets him stay in his dog house and he feeds him. But the other boy teaches his puppy tricks and how to hunt. Now, J.J., which puppy do you think will be more useful to a man who owns a zoo?

J.J.

The puppy that is trained to do tricks and hunt!

PATRICIA

Very good, J.J. In our world, J.J., there are lots of people. Some people's skin is like mine – we say white.

Patricia rolls up her sleeves and lets J.J. see her hands and arms and says –

PATRICIA (CONT'D)

Now look at your hands and arms –

J.J. looks at his hands and arms and Patricia says –

PATRICIA (CONT'D)

Now, you see, your hands and arms are a different color than mine.

J.J. smiles and says –

J.J.

Yeah, mama, I can see. My hands and arms are black.

PATRICIA

Indeed, J.J. so who is superior or better, you or I?

J.J.

Neither one of us, mama!

PATRICIA

But J.J. I can drive a car and cook, but you can't. Doesn't that make me better than you?

J.J.

But mama, could you always drive a car and cook?

PATRICIA

No, J.J. I could not always drive a car nor cook.

J.J.

When I get older and bigger, I will be able to drive a car and learn how to cook, too.

PATRICIA

Then, you say that I'm not smarter nor better than you.

J.J.

That's right, mama.

PATRICIA

You are right, J.J. What we are and who we are cannot be measured by the color of our skin nor by what we can do, because if we try, all of us can do what anybody else can do.

The scene closes. The scene opens as J.J. and Patricia are down town and J.J. says –

J.J.

Mama, I'm hungry! Can I have a sandwich?

PATRICIA

Surely, you can, J.J.

Patricia takes J.J. and they go into: "Hungry Eatery" and take a seat. There are only a few people in the Eatery, so, Patricia says to J.J. –

PATRICIA

Ok, J.J. you can have a hot dog and some chips! How is that?

J.J.

Good, mama.

After sitting almost five minutes and nobody has come to take their order, Patricia raps on the table. One waiter sees her and says to the Manager, Jack Kemp –

WAITER

Jack, what do I do?

JACK

Just show her the sign.

WAITER

I recognize her! Do you know who she is?

JACK

Don't know and could care less – watch me so that next time you will know what to do!

Jack walks over to the table where J.J. and Patricia are seated and says –

JACK

Mam, you are welcome to make an order, but that boy can't eat in here!

PATRICIA

And why not?

JACK

Mam, he's a Negro.

PATRICIA

Do I look like I am a Negro?

JACK

No mam, but that boy does and he can't eat in here!

PATRICIA

I'm his mother and he can eat whenever and wherever I eat!

JACK

Sorry, mam!

Jack walks away. Patricia gets up and walks over and knocks on the door with a sign that reads: Owner. The Owner, Tim Randolph, answers the door-

TIM

Mam, can I help you?

PATRICIA

I am not sure, but I see business is a bit slow! What's the problem?

TIM

Mam, I wish I knew – business is way off.

PATRICIA

Why don't you sell the place?

TIM

Make me an offer!

Patricia takes out her check book and says –

PATRICIA

How much and how shall I write the check?

Tim is shocked, but quite pleased and says –

TIM

I'll take five thousand – make the check payable to: Tim Randolph.

Patricia writes the check, gives it to Tim and says –

PATRICIA

How would you like to be my Manager?

TIM

Fine!

PATRICIA

Call all your workers out here.

TIM

Yes, mam!

Tim calls all the workers and exclaims –

TIM

I just sold this place to this lady. She is your new boss.

Patricia looks at the workers and doesn't see Jack and the waiter and says –

PATRICIA

Where are Jack and that waiter with the yellow apron?

Tim calls them and they rush out of the kitchen. Patricia looks them over and says –

PATRICIA

Fire them! Both of them!

JACK

But Mam, I need to work!

PATRICIA

You are supposed to serve people, but you chose not to serve my son and me, so you are fired and anybody else who wants to go!

Patricia looks to Tim and says –

PATRICIA

Tim, have a nice sign out there that reads "Members Only." Membership fee is five cents. Now somebody bring my son a hot dog, some chips, a soda and me a glass of lemonade! Oh, change – The name of this place to: "Anybody's Can Eat Eatery!"

Two days later, Patricia and J.J. visit the restaurant across the street. She and J.J. walk in and take a seat. No waiter comes to serve them. Patricia raps on the table and the Manager, Bob Taylor, comes to her table –

BOB

Mam, I'm sorry, but we don't serve Colored!

PATRICIA

Good! I'm white, so you can serve me!

BOB

Yes, mam, I can serve you, but not that boy!

PATRICIA

That boy happens to be my son. And he eats whenever and wherever I eat! And if you have any objections, call the owner for me!

Bob is aware what happened to the "Hungry Eatery" across the street and says –

BOB

Mam, if I serve you, I might get fired!

PATRICIA

If you don't serve me, you will get fired!

In fright, Bob has a waiter to take Patricia's order and they are served. As Patricia is about to leave, she calls Bob, gives him a fifty dollar tip and says –

PATRICIA

Young man, always do what's right and just, even if it means going against a rule. And God will bless you!

Now Patricia and J.J. stops in any restaurant in that Plaza and are served. The scene closes and opens as Patricia and J.J. have First Class seats reserve on Alstana Airways. Patricia and J.J. board the plane and go to their seats. Shortly, thereafter, a stewardess accosts Patricia –

STEWARDESS

I'm sorry, Mam, but that boy cannot sit here!

PATRICIA

And please tell me why not?

Holding her ticket up for the stewardess to see, Patricia says –

PATRICIA

I have two First Class seats! Put me off if you wish, and I'll sue this Airline for a million dollars!

The stewardess goes and talks with the Captain and never returns. Patricia becomes quite active in Civil Rights Movements. The scene closes and opens at Patricia's parents' home –

MR. FOXX

Pat, I see that you have been quite active in matters that I don't think should concern you. People have a right to decide how they will operate their businesses.

PATRICIA

Really, daddy! You have always talked about justice. But daddy, is it right for J.J. or any child be hungry and not be sold a sandwich because he's black? I never knew nor thought you meant just for the rich and well-to-do!

MR. FOXX

I didn't make the Laws! And meddling unnecessarily won't make things better.

MRS. FOXX

Jul, I am sorry to hear you say that. John Burke said, "All is necessary for evil to triumph for good people to nothing." He was right! There comes a time when we have to stand for what we know darn well is right.

PATRICIA

If people are allowed to do what they please, soon what they do wrong, will be right to them.

Patricia looks at her parents and says –

PATRICIA (CONT'D)

Mama you and daddy and all mamas and daddies in Allen County and other Allen Counties have perpetuated injustice! Yes, I know, daddy, you and mama have been just with Negroes, but you have not tried to encourage your neighbors to follow suit! And that's a sin of omission, daddy.

It's silence for a few moments and Mr. Foxx exclaims –

MR. FOXX

To that, I agree. But what can one person fighting alone and against thousands can do?

MRS. FOXX

You'll never know unless you try!

MR. FOXX

Deep within, Pat and Til, I know you are right. But I'm too far down the road to worry about it.

PATRICIA

Not really, daddy. People in this County highly respect you and your opinion. Why don't you try!

MR. FOXX

Maybe so! Maybe So!

Then, Mr. Foxx reminds Pat about his meeting with leading persons in the County to discuss matters to promote goodwill among the races, and she is delighted!

The scene closes and opens. Mr. Troy Bench is in Judge Harry Baker's Chamber discussing with him about filing charges against Patricia for letting whites and Negroes eat in her business: "Anybody's Eatery." Troy says –

TROY

Judge, it isn't fair; I'm losing customers!

JUDGE

Troy, what she is doing is perfectly legal. It's a Private Club.

TROY

Judge everybody knows that, that is a hoax!

JUDGE

Maybe so, but it's legal. And by the way the Owner knows what's legal – she should! She is a Summa Cum Laude Law graduate of one of the finest Law Schools in this nation.

TROY

Then I had better try a different angle.

JUDGE

Fine, but what angle is there?

TROY

I'll buy her out!

Judge Baker chuckles and Troy remarks –

TROY

I don't know what's funny about buying her out, Judge. I'll offer her a price that she can't refuse.

Judge Baker really chuckles and Troy retorts –

TROY

Judge, maybe you know something that I don't.

JUDGE

Must be!

On a serious note, Judge Baker looks at Troy and says –

JUDGE (CONT'D)

Mr. Bench, Patricia Smith, no doubt, has a balance in her checking account twice the size of your total assets, and you talking about making her an offer that she can't refuse – that's what I chuckled about!

Judge Baker pauses and softly says –

JUDGE (CONT'D)

Mr. Bench, I been on the Bench for years – things are changing, fellow! Antiquated thoughts and ideas of yesterday must yield and concede to today's thoughts and ideas! Yes, just like the mule and plow had to yield to the tractor; and the horse and buggy had to yield to the automobile. Things are changing, and if we don't accept these changes and adjust to these changes, we might just become obsolete!

TROY

I guess I hadn't considered it that way, Judge. Maybe you're right!

JUDGE

No maybe about it – It's a fact. Why do you think we don't have dinosaurs but whales? I'll tell you: The dinosaurs couldn't adjust but the whale did!

TROY

Judge, this has truly been a good lesson for me and an eye opener! So glad I came. But rest assured that I am a different Troy leaving than when I came and for the better!

The scene closes as Troy and Judge Baker shake hands.

J.J. is six years old now and has begun to wonder more about his color as it relates to him and his mother. Talking to his mama, he says –

J.J.

Mama, I see you and daddy high school pictures and both of you are white. Then, why am I black?

Patricia goes to her bookshelf and takes off of it a book that contains just birds and she turns to some white swans and says –

PATRICIA

What is the name of this bird, J.J.?

J.J. smiles and says –

                    J.J.

Mama, everybody knows that is a swan.

                 PATRICIA

Right you are, J.J. What color are they?

                    J.J.

Mama, they are white.

                 PATRICIA

Right you are again, J.J.

Then Patricia turns to a page of black swans and says –

             PATRICIA (CONT'D)

J.J. what is the name of these birds?

J.J. looks for a few seconds and says –

                    J.J.

Oh, mama, they are swans, too.

                 PATRICIA

What color are they, J.J.?

J.J. smiles and responds –

                    J.J.

Why, they are black, mama.

PATRICIA

For a long time, J.J. we thought all swans <u>was</u> white. Somewhere along the way, God must have decided to make some swans black. But nobody really knows why. I think that's what happened to your dad and me. We don't know why, but God must have decided that it was time for a white couple to have a black baby boy!

J.J.

Gee, mama, I'm so glad God chose you for my mama!

The scene closes. J.J. is enrolled at Robinsville Elementary and the scene opens at his Arithmetic Class. The teacher, Mrs. Mary Swinson, is speaking –

MRS. SWINSON

Class, today we are going to understand more about our number line. You will need to know this when you take Algebra in the eighth grade.

J.J. raises his hand and Mrs. Swinson acknowledges him –

MRS. SWINSON (CONT'D)

Ok, J.J. what's your concern?

                    J.J.

Mrs. Swinson, there are interesting properties about the number line that teachers don't tell us!

                 MRS. SWINSON

Like what, J.J.?

                    J.J.

Starting to left of zero, and going right, what is the first number between 0 and 1?

One boy, Bobby Benton, yells out –

                   BOBBY

That's simple, Mrs. Swinson!

                    J.J.

Ok, Bobby, then what is the number?

It's silent for a few moments, then Bobby yells –

                   BOBBY

It's one! That's right, one!

                 MRS. SWINSON

Bobby, that cannot be correct, because one-half comes before one!

A girl, Patty Rush, yells out –

PATTY

I know, Mrs. Swinson. It's one-third.

J.J.

Well, Patty, one-sixth is smaller than one-third. So that can't be the answer.

This goes on for a while, then one student, Raymond Smith, says –

RAYMOND

Then tell us J.J., what is the first number between zero and one?

J.J. pauses for a few moments and one boy, Mel yells –

MEL

J.J. doesn't know either, Mrs. Swinson!

Mrs. Swinson looks at J.J. and says –

MRS. SWINSON

Want to tell us, J.J.?

J.J.

Yes, Mam! There is no first number between zero and one!

A girl, Betty yells –

BETTY

Yes, it is! Yes, it is!

MRS. SWINSON

Ok, Betty, then tell the class what is the first number between zero and one?

BETTY

It's zero.

MRS. SWINSON

J.J. said between zero and one, Betty!

Mrs. Swinson looks to J.J. and says –

MRS. SWINSON

Ok, J.J. tell the class why there is no first number between zero and one.

J.J.

Suppose you say that K is the first number between zero and one, then I say $0 < K/2 < K$. So K was not the first number between zero and one.

A boy, Billy, yells –

BILLY

Yeah, but what is K, J.J.?

J.J.

Any number you want it to be, so long as it's between zero and one. I'll just take one-half of that number and get a smaller number!

MRS. SWINSON

Indeed, J.J. that is a wonder property of our number line and there are others.

A girl, Ann, yells –

ANN

Tell us some more, J.J.!

MRS. SWINSON

No, not today! We will let J.J. give us another one next week.

The scene closes and opens and Patricia and J.J.'s homeroom Teacher, Mrs. Raychel Adams, are in conference. Mrs. Adams is speaking –

MRS. ADAMS

Mrs. Smith, J.J. is a jewel. He is unusually bright and gifted and my students enjoy feeding off his genius!

PATRICIA

I am so delighted to hear that, and feel so blessed that he is so well accepted.

MRS. ADAMS

Indeed, here at Robinsville, we are committed to the education of all students irrespective to race, color or creed!

The scene fast-forwards to the conclusion of Patricia's and Mrs. Adams Conference –

MRS. ADAMS

Yes, it is a privilege to have J.J. in my class. His brilliance makes me read, myself. He has a sense of curiosity that is too often missing. Most students can excel if motivated to do so.

PATRICIA

J.J. is a good boy, and I knew that he would not cause any trouble – I just wondered how he would be received by the other children.

MRS. ADAMS

Mrs. Smith, children learn what they live. The racial problem in this nation could be radically changed overnight if parents and other adults will it so. Kids learn from their parents. And if parents would act and talk justice and fair play, this is exactly what their kids would learn and display.

PATRICIA

Makes good sense to me!

MRS. ADAMS

So, we teachers, just treat all our students the same, and the kids take their clues from us.

PATRICIA

I am happy that we had this chat, Mrs. Adams, and thanks a million.

The scene closes as Mrs. Adams and Patricia shake hands. The scene opens in J.J.'s Political Science Class in Robinsville High. J.J. is a senior. The teacher, Mr. Dave Patterson, is talking –

MR. PATTERSON

Who can tell me where is the birthplace of democracy?

Lots of hands go up and Mr. Patterson points to a girl, Naomi Swain, and says –

MR. PATTERSON

Ok, Ms. Na, Na, tell us.

NAOMI

In Athens, Greece.

MR. PATTERSON

Indeed, Na Na, Athens, Greece. What was unique about the first form of democracy?

J.J. raises his hand and Mr. Patterson says –

MR. PATTERSON (CONT'D)

Ok, J.J., let's have your take.

J.J.

It was said to be a pure case of democracy, because everyone could vote in one setting.

MR. PATTERSON

Correct, J.J. But with millions of people voting as we have here in America makes a pure democracy virtually impossible. Which is better a democratic government? Or an oligarchy?

A student, Marcel Winston, raises her hand. Mr. Patterson recognizes her and says –

MR. PATTERSON (CONT'D)

Ok, Marcel, let's hear your response.

MARCEL

In an oligarchy, the decisions about the governance of the nation are entrusted to a few persons.

Mr. Patterson cuts in and says –

MR. PATTERSON

What's wrong with a few people making all decisions? It certainly would be far less

MR. PATTERSON (CONT'D)

expensive to operate an oligarchy than a democracy!

J.J. responds –

J.J.

True, Mr. Patterson, but a few people cannot express the will of the whole. I think President Abraham Lincoln was right when he proposed a government of the people, for the people and by the people!

MR. PATTERSON

Well said, J.J. But what is the psychological impact our form of government has?

J.J.

People are far more supportive of matters that express their views and concerns, and can accept the negative consequences much better.

MR. PATTERSON

Indeed! If we are going on a class trip and I make all the decisions and we get there and don't like it, I then must bear the burden all by myself. But, if everyone has input, then we all share in the disappointment and nobody is to blame.

A student, Fred Peacox, raises his hand and Mr. Patterson recognizes him –

MR. PATTERSON

Very well, Fred, let's hear from you.

FRED

We have a democratic government. Yet, there are those who wish to control and influence the vote in their best interest. In an oligarchy, we wouldn't have this kind of "foul play."

MR. PATTERSON

I agree, Fred. But in a democracy, the people are privileged to go to the polls and vote those kinds of persons out of office.

FRED

But, Mr. Patterson, so many people won't go to the polls and vote!

MR. PATTERSON

That is correct, Fred. But the good thing is that they can go and it is always possible to persuade them to go and vote. But in an oligarchy, most people are not given that choice.

The scene fast-forwards to the conclusion of the class and Mr. Patterson exclaims –

MR. PATTERSON (CONT'D)

Class, this has been a very enjoyable discourse, and I think we all got a lot from it. Just think if the rules of this class were such that only three of you were permitted to voice your opinions. I don't think the class would be nearly as interesting and as beneficial.

The scene closes and opens at Robinsville International Airport. John just flew in from La, and as he is getting in his rental car, Patricia passes in her car and recognizes him. She pulls over and watches him from her rearview mirror.

PATRICIA

(Soliloquizing)

I wish he would see me and stop! But what would we talk about? Maybe I should get out of the car and open the trunk and maybe he will see me as he passes.

John signs the papers that the car delivery person gives him and drives off and as he passes by Patricia as he thinks he can be heard –

JOHN

(Soliloquy)

Just think of all the times I used to arrive from trips and Pat would be here to pick me up! Life was so wonderful and exciting with her that it

JOHN (CONT'D)

(Soliloquy)

seems as if I were in heaven before my time! Deep down within, I knew Pat would never be unfaithful to me! Why on God's earth didn't I accept the boy! God answers prayers, but not always exactly as we wish them to be answered. How ungrateful! Ungrateful could I have been!

The scene switches to Patricia still sitting in her car –

PATRICIA

(Soliloquy)

Why couldn't I have been here to pick up John? Oh, God! We prayed for a child and God answered our prayer, but John wouldn't accept His answer! Why, John? Why! Why, John! We could have made it work! I know you could have been as proud of J.J. as I am. We were special to each other, John! And why do we have to live in separate worlds – separate worlds, in reality but not in spirit. You'll always be my world; my all; my everything!! John, we live in a world that has eclipsed.

The scene closes and opens the next day at 9 A.M. John is at a CEO Meeting at the Homebase of the Enterprise.

                   JOHN

Folks, it's good to be back at the old "stumping ground." And I have nothing but good news to report.

John has the Secretary and Recorder to pass out some financial documents.

              JOHN (CONT'D)

This year has been another "banner year." Profits have "skyrocketed." They have never been better!

Looking at the head CEO and good friend, RaMon Sanderson, John remarks –

                   JOHN

RaMon has maximized efficiency in every aspect of the company. Each of you has done a superb job in your own area of specialization. I'm proud to have you onboard!

The scene fast-forwards and John is concluding his remarks –

                   JOHN

Again, thanks guys for a job well done! Are there any questions or expressions of concern that I need to entertain?

RAMON

I would just like to say that we here at the home base are genuinely pleased and gratified that everything here is up and beyond par. Next year, we'll be shooting for and "eagle."

The scene closes and opens at a class in Calculus that J.J. is taking in the "Co-op Program." The teacher is Dr. Ryan Goodwin. J.J. raises his hand and Dr. Goodwin says –

DR. GOODWIN

Ok, Mr. J.J. what have you for us today that is of unusual interest?

J.J.

Professor Goodwin, we are discussing the behavior of certain functions: Bending points or points of inflection and relative minimum and maximum, and continuity. If we were to plug a whole in the number line, for instance, suppose the number five was plucked out of the number line, how would that change the characteristic of the line?

DR. GOODWIN

There would just be a hole in the line! I don't see how that would change the character of the line, do you?

Dr. Goodwin knows the answer but wants to let J.J. respond –

J.J.

I was reading in a book called Real Analysis and it said that between any two real number, there is another real number. And he said that makes the line densed, but if I pluck the number 5 out of that line, that would grossly affect certain functions. A function continues at the number 5 would no longer be continuous there, etc.

DR. GOODWIN

Good thinking, J.J. I teach a class in Real Analysis and I think you should take it.

J.J.

Thanks, Sir. I will consider that.

The scene closes and opens and Mrs. Rich (the Lady who vehemently opposed J.J.'s admission to Robinsville Elementary) and two friends, Mrs. Margrett Brown and Mary Dykes, are finishing having tea at the Palatial Inn are about to leave for home. Mrs. Rich remarks –

MRS. RICH

Are there any good news we should share?

MRS. DYKES

Yes, indeed! Pat, our oldest son, is finally making the "Honor Roll." There is some student at Robinsville High who volunteers to tutor students who are having problems in that Algebra II! Gee, it's a blessing.

MRS. RICH

Our son Roger is also in that group.

MRS. BROWN

And Alex is in there, too. And it's a "God Send." Frank paid a tutor several dollars an hour to tutor Roger –

Mrs. Brown bursts out in a big laugh and says –

MRS. BROWN (CONT'D)

And got pass the "D" category.

MRS. RICH

That was the same with Roger. We had him a tutor in Algebra I and Algebra II, but to no avail.

MRS. DYKES

All I can say is: Ditto!

MRS. RUSH

This student, Ahmad, must be some teacher!

MRS. DYKES

Yeah! He should have some of those Mathematics teachers in his sessions so they could learn how to teach!

MRS. BROWN

Amen!

The three ladies decide to stop by the Library Annex where J.J. is tutoring. After the divorce, Patricia changed J.J. name to: Ahmad (J.J.) Smith. However, on all legal documents, J.J. just lists his name as Ahmad Smith. Mrs. Rich, Brown and Dykes arrive at the Annex and the scene depicts them being directed to where J.J. tutors. Mrs. Rich accosts J.J. and says –

MRS. RICH

Boy, these ladies and I are looking for our sons. Roger, Pat and Alex. They are supposed to be here for tutoring. Do you know them?

J.J.

Yes, Mam! They are running a bit late. They had a meeting with their basketball Coach.

MRS. RICH

Ok!

Mrs. Rich goes back to where Mrs. Brown and Mrs. Dykes are seated and says –

MRS. RICH

That boy over there said that Roger, Pat and Alex had a meeting with their basketball Coach and running a bit late. I guess he is being tutored also!

MRS. BROWN

No doubt that he needs to be! It's annoying how things have changed.

MRS. DYKES

And for the better, I think!

MRS. RICH

There you go again, Bettye! You were always against the status quo!

MRS. DYKES

And should be when the status quo is out of kilter with justice!

MRS. RICH

By whose scale of Justice, Bettye?

The scene depicts Roger, Pat and Alex rushing through the door and Roger yells to J.J. –

ROGER

Ahmad, we apologize for being late!

J.J.

That's ok, fellows! I'm fine.

Roger, Pat and Alex stop to talk with their moms –

ROGER

Mama, what brought you all by here?

MRS. RICH

We thought we'd come by and show our gratitude to the kind and thoughtful young man who is making the sacrifice to tutor you three.

MRS. DYKES

And free of charge!

MRS. BROWN

He is truly a Good Samaritan!

Mrs. Rich, with a supercilious look, says –

MRS. RICH

That boy over there told us why you all were detained.

Looking around, Mrs. Rich says –

MRS. RICH (CONT'D)

Where is your tutor – Ahmad, I believe you call him?

Roger, pointing to J.J., says –

ROGER

That's him over there, mama!

Mrs. Rich and Mrs. Dykes are awestruck!

MRS. DYKES

What?

PAT

He saved us and helped us to get on the "Honor Roll."

It's silent for a moment, then Mrs. Brown says –

MRS. BROWN

Boys, we thought we would offer your tutor a small financial award.

Pat chuckles and Mrs. Dykes says to him –

MRS. DYKES

And what on earth is there to chuckle about, Pat?

PAT

His mom is a multi-millionaire!

Roger says, come on mama, let us introduce you all to Ahmad! They walk over to J.J. and Roger says –

ROGER

Ahmad, these ladies are our moms –

Pointing, Roger says –

ROGER (CONT'D)

My mom, Mrs. Bettye Rich; Mrs. Margaret Brown, Alex's mom; and Mrs. Mary Dykes, Pat's mom.

J.J. politely bows and says –

J.J.

Ladies, it's a pleasure to meet you. You have three wonderful sons. It's nothing wrong with their abilities to learn. Somewhere along life's journey, they were given false and untrue opinions about Mathematics. As you know, I am sure; the real truth about anything is in the mind of the beholder. I understand that the notorious gangster, John Dillinger, carved a fake pistol from a piece of wood and used black shoe polish to give the wood a metal effect and used it to force the man on guard duty to free him from his cell. Thus, believing that Mathematics was difficult, your sons approached it as though it was!

MRS. BROWN

Well said, young man. Many people live distorted lives due to false views. We came to

MRS. BROWN (CONT'D)

reward you but, instead, you have rewarded us beyond words! You blessed us!

The scene fast-forwards and the mothers are about to leave. J.J. reaches out and shakes their hands and Mrs. Brown says –

MRS. BROWN

We mothers came by to offer you a small and modest financial taken to express our profound gratitude for what you have done for our sons.

J.J.

It was my pleasure, Mam!

The scene closes and opens as Mrs. Brown, Mrs. Rich and Mrs. Dykes are enroute home.

MRS. BROWN

Bettye, what do you two women have to say about the tutor?

MRS. DYKES

Really, what is there to say? There are always exceptions!

MRS. RICH

No, Mary! It's one thing to be wrong and not know it. But it's unforgivable to be wrong and

MRS. RICH (CONT'D)

aware of it and not admit it. Naturally, I cannot change a lifetime of behavior in a moment, but I can accept the truth in a moment!

MRS. BROWN

Exactly! Absolutely! We had an experience that defies much of what we were taught by precept and example all of our lives. And let's face it, that Ahmad was the epitome of excellence in every respect.

MRS. DYKES

Well –

MRS. RICH

Well, nothing! Let's face it Mary, I wish Roger were as articulate as that young man! Just face the facts – no one is asking you to invite him to dinner, though I would, all we are saying is face the truth! I am personally, going back to my school and apologize to my colleagues and write that mom a letter and tell her how blessed she is to have such a wonderful son and apologize for my stupidity rather, for my parents and other adults stupidity!

The scene closes and opens and J.J. has finished high school and employed with Watts Industries, a Subsidiary of Smith's Enterprises, Inc., located in Spokecane,

Washington. J.J. has been employed with Watts Industries for five years and has received the best evaluations of any person in the firm since its beginning. He has a meeting in La with John (his father). They are in dialogue.

JOHN

Ahmad, I reviewed your record very, very careful and I am convinced that you are the person to take the lead position as CEO in Robinsville, East Virginia. You are being asked to fill some "big shoes." My best friend, RaMon Sanderson, has decided to retire from that position and work on a part-time basis. Do you think you can fill the post?

AHMAD (J.J.)

Well, Mr. Smith, I accepted your offer and, unless I was absolutely certain that I could, I would not have accepted your offer. My work is a portrait of me, and that has to be "top flight."

JOHN

I like confidence! But over-confidence can be a liability.

AHMAD

Yes, Sir! And a lack of confidence can be a disaster!

The scene fast-forwards and comes to the conclusion of the interview –

JOHN

I see that you are from Robinsville. That's my home, too. What high school did you attend?

AHMAD

Robinsville High.

JOHN

That school replaced my old high school – Allen County High. Well, we have one thing in common – last names.

AHMAD

Yes, Sir! That is correct!

JOHN

Do you have any siblings? Or you like me, the Loney!

AHMAD

Yes, Sir, I am my mom's only child.

JOHN

I note that you said: My mom's only child! What about your father?

AHMAD

Well, Sir, that's a bit of a mystery!

JOHN

I gather the ties between you and your father are broken!

AHMAD

Really, my father and I never really had a tie.

JOHN

Well, that's on a personal note, and I should not go down that way!

The scene closes and during the six weeks of briefing, John and Ahmad (J.J.) spend lots of time together having lunch, attending workshops, etc. They have really gotten to be closely nitched. The scene depicts J.J. on the phone with Patricia –

PATRICIA

J.J., I am delighted that you have gotten promoted to CEO in such a short time. To God be the Glory!

J.J.

Yes, Mama, it's a blessing. I, am delighted. And guess where I am going to work?

PATRICIA

I don't know, but I hope your job isn't being outsourced to Japan or somewhere!

J.J.

Not quite that far, mama. That's too far from home!

PATRICIA

Spokane is far enough! Overseas, and I would see you once every "blue moon!" But just tell me!

J.J.

Hold your breath!

PATRICIA

Ok, J.J. I am holding my breath, where?

J.J.

Robinsville! Yes, Robinsville!

Patricia is hysteric and yells –

PATRICIA

Hallelujah! When do you report to work?

J.J.

I am in training and I'll complete it in six weeks and stay here for a brief period. So I would say in about two months.

PATRICIA

That was the job interview you mentioned, I guess?

J.J.

Right!

PATRICIA

How did it go? Good, I'm sure!

J.J.

Yes, indeed. The big boss and I had a "merry go round." We hit it big! I really like him and he seems to really like me, too!

PATRICIA

That's good, J.J.

The scene closes and Patricia is at home visiting her parents.

PATRICIA

Guess what daddy? You, too, Mama.

MRS. FOXX

Pat, without any clue, how are we to know how to begin? Give us a clue!

PATRICIA

Your grandson is being promoted to CEO! Yes, CEO!

MR. FOXX

I say Amen to that and hallelujah! That boy has good blood in him!

MRS. FOXX

Yes, my blood.

Everyone has a good old fashion Lol!

MR. FOXX

Where will he be headquartered, Pat? Too often when one is promoted to CEO, he's off to China or somewhere.

MRS. FOXX

God forbid!

PATRICIA

No sweat! No sweat!

MRS. FOXX

Then, tell us, child!

PATRICIA

To Robinsville!

MR. FOXX

That's good news!

It's silent for a few moments, then Mr. Foxx says –

MR. FOXX (CONT'D)

The Bible says that God works in mysterious ways and indeed, he does! I often look back on those days when that child was born and think, for a spell, how narrow-sighted I was.

PATRICIA

Yes, daddy, those were trying times. I deeply regret that John's parents – really his father - never could bring himself to accept J.J.

MRS. FOXX

Yeah! But Teresa felt ok about the matter. But you know, James is so domineering that she could not do what deep within she wanted to do.

PATRICIA

Well, I can understand the road she took. Too, if John had accepted J.J., in due season, both of his parents would have come over to our side.

MR. FOXX

Indeed, life is queer with its twists and turns as all of us sometimes learns!

MRS. FOXX

Too often, we let the social status quo determine our way of life, even when that way of life is contrary to justice!

PATRICIA

You know, mama, daddy, I really don't hold any feelings of hatred toward them. Just supposed J.J. were a white boy and I had been raised in the Southern tradition as we, John and I, were and his, J.J.'s, wife, gave birth to a black baby boy. How would I have reacted – I really don't know but the odds are that I would have reacted the way John and his parents reacted- irrational, yes! But the real fault does not lie with John, but with his parents, their parents and back and back it goes.

MR. FOXX

You are right, Pat. Our beliefs are expressions of what we learned from our parents and the environment in which we were raised.

MRS. FOXX

I wonder what made the first white person who felt that he or she was better than Negroes to feel that way. I just wonder!

MR. FOXX

It's hard to say. It seems as if it were an inheritance.

The scene ends and J.J. (Ahmad) and John are on connecting flights to Robinsville. They are enjoying the flight and in dialogue –

JOHN

Well, Ahmad, I know that a million thoughts are going through your mind. That's normal, but it will be ok!

AHMAD (J.J.)

That is correct. Believe it, or not, but lots of people have a greater fear for making changes from one position to another than the fear of death. But, I'm ok.

JOHN

You said that your mom is picking you up. I could drop you off.

AHMAD

Thanks, but she gets a kick at seeing her son walking down airport corridors like a professional!

JOHN

Your mom seems like a terrific person.

AHMAD

Indeed! She has always been the "Winds beneath my wings."

JOHN

Her winds must have the power of a Tsunami. It got you from a beginner to CEO in less than five years! That's some power!

AHMAD

Yes, I agree!

It's silent for a few moments and John can sense that Ahmad is holding something back and says –

JOHN

I sense that you want to ask me something. Go right ahead and ask me.

AHMAD

Yes, you are correct, I do.

JOHN

Then, shoot!

AHMAD

Such a nice man like yourself, I cannot help but wonder if you were ever married – gosh, almost any woman would be pleased and happy to have such a man for a husband and any child would be happy and blessed to have you for a father.

John shows gestures of Ahmad's comments and says –

JOHN

Ahmad, my son, that's a long story – a long story. In due time, I'll have to tell you about it!

AHMAD

Sounds good to me, and I take a "rain check."

Both John and Ahmad have a good old Lol and the Pilot comes on –

PILOT

Ladies and Gentlemen, this your Captain, we will be landing at Robinsville International Airport very shortly. At this time, we ask all passengers to please fasten your seatbelts and put all cell phones and other electronic devices in the "off position." It has been our pleasure to have you aboard Melta Flight 299 and we hope to see you

PILOT (CONT'D)

again on one of Melta Flights. Have a pleasant stay in the Robinsville Area. The plane lands and the scene depicts John and Ahmad walking down the corridor. Ahmad takes out his phone and dials Patricia; she answers –

PATRICIA

Hello, J.J. this is mom I guess you are here!

J.J.

Yes, mom, we just landed and are on our way to the baggage pick-up.

PATRICIA

You said, we; is someone with you?

J.J.

Oh, yes, mom, my boss.

PATRICIA

Good, now I'll get to meet him.

As John and Ahmad (J.J.) are walking down the corridor, they get an attention notice.

VOICE

This call is for a Mr. John Smith. You left your laptop on Melta Flight 299. Please return and get it.

JOHN

Ahmad, you heard that! Gee, how careless and forgetful! Never happened before.

Looking at Ahmad, John says –

JOHN (CONT'D)

Ahmad, go ahead and don't keep your mom waiting. I'll only be a few minutes behind you.

John turns to go back to Melta Flight 299 to claim his laptop. The scene depicts J.J. and Patricia seeing each other and both rush to embrace –

PATRICIA

Gosh, J.J., it's so good to see you!

J.J.

Yes, indeed, mama. Dorothy, in the Wizard of Oz, was right: "There's no place like home!"

As Patricia and J.J. talk, John rings J.J.

JOHN

Ahmad, these people know that this laptop is mine, but I have to go through their rigmarole to get it and it might take from a half-hour to an hour to do so. I don't want you and your mom standing and waiting for me. Go on home and we'll all have lunch one day –ok?

AHMAD

As you say, John, but it won't be any problem to wait.

JOHN

I know, but just go ahead. I don't want you to have to wait.

AHMAD

Ok, John.

Patricia looks at J.J. and asks –

PATRICIA

What was that all about, J.J.?

J.J.

You know, I told you that John left his laptop on the plane and went to get it. But it seems as if he has to go through lots of rigmarole to get it and he doesn't want to hold us up.

PATRICIA

I don't mind!

J.J.

I know, mama, but John hates to think he's a bother. He said that the three of us can have lunch one day.

PATRICIA

Sounds like a winner to me, J.J.

The scene closes as J.J. gets his luggage and he and Patricia are in their car enroute home.

The scene opens at a staff meeting and RaMon is about to introduce Ahmad.

RAMON

My friends, these are moments of ambivalence for me! For more than twenty years, I have had the good pleasure to be an integral part of this wonderful Enterprise. And fifteen years as it's leader her at the home office.

RaMon is almost in tears and pauses for a few moments and resumes his talk.

RAMON

Today, I officially step down as your leader and pass the baton to our new CEO, Ahmad Smith.

Looking at John, RaMon says –

RAMON (CONT'D)

He passed the scrutiny test of John and that says a lot! Indeed, Ahmad is duly qualified to lead us to even greater heights. Naturally, I'll still be looking over your shoulders –

Everyone has a good Lol, and RaMon continues –

                    RAMON (CONT'D)

So, without further ado, let's receive our new boss, Mr. Ahmad Smith –

Everyone stands and gives Ahmad a warm round of applause as he steps forth –

                    AHMAD

Thank you, RaMon, for that fine introduction and you my colleagues for that warm welcome. "Heights by Great Men reached and kept were not obtained by sudden flight, but they while their companions slept were toiling upward through the night." Indeed, I am blessed and honored to have been chosen to head Smith Enterprises here at Robinsville, my home site,

Ahmad turns and looks at RaMon and comments –

                    AHMAD (CONT'D)

You have had "top flight" leadership and guidance under the awesome leadership of RaMon Sanderson, and I promise to sustain that high quality leadership as we continue to toil upward through the night.

Everyone stands and applauds and Ahmad continues –

                    AHMAD (CONT'D)

Ladies and Gentlemen, a good leader does not attempt to lead from behind with a whip, but in

AHMAD (CONT'D)

front with a banner! A leader cannot lift himself to success; he must be lifted by the persons he leads. And a weak and inefficient group cannot lift him, and a dissatisfied group will refuse to lift him. We are a team and we will function as a team. I will not have the answers to all of the questions we must ask nor the solution to all of the problems we must solve. But working together, we will answer those questions; working together, we will solve those problems. Yes, together we will reach higher plateaus, fathom deeper depths and explore new frontiers. Yes, we will continue in the great tradition that has made Smith Enterprises the best and keep it the best! God bless each of you; God bless Smith Enterprises; and God bless America!

Everyone stands and cheers. The scene closes as John shakes Ahmad's hand and embraces him and says –

JOHN

It's a genuine pleasure to have you aboard, Ahmad! Smith Enterprises is still in good hands! I wish your mom could have been here; she would have been proud of you!

The scene opens two weeks later and Patricia is going by J.J.'s office to take him some papers he forgot and left on his desk and to have lunch. She arrives and J.J. is about to leave for a brief meeting.

J.J.

Hi, mom! Got to run to this meeting. Be back shortly!

PATRICIA

That's ok, J.J. I'll just sit here and read.

J.J. is off to his meeting and John stops by his office. He sees Patricia, but she has her back to him and says –

JOHN

Pardon me, Mam, I'm looking for Ahmad.

Patricia recognizes his voice and turns and both are startled!

PATRICIA

John, oh, my God!

JOHN

Pat, Goodness sake! What on earth are you doing here?

PATRICIA

I just stopped by to see my son, J.J.

JOHN

But this is Ahmad's Office!

It's silent for a moment, as John and Patricia both seem to be speechless! They walk close to each other and hold hands –

JOHN

My God, Pat! Can this be real!

As they stand there staring in each other's eyes, the music and words of the song: "Impossible" can be heard!

PATRICIA

John, you look wonderful, just as I remembered you for the past twenty plus years!

JOHN

And you too – just as I have remembered you for the past twenty plus years!

PATRICIA

I waited a lifetime for you to call; to write or anything!

JOHN

And not a single day in all these twenty plus years have I not wanted to!

Both, John and Patricia, can see in each other's eyes and facial expressions that their love for each other is still intact and indestructible!

JOHN (CONT'D)

And Ahmad – J.J.

PATRICIA

Yes, John! That's our son.

JOHN

Yes, Pat! Yes Pat, our Son!

PATRICIA

Yes, and he's such a fine young man – just like his daddy!

JOHN

Yes, he is a fine young man – like me, I don't know!

PATRICIA

Like you, yes!

Patricia looks at John, smiles and says –

PATRICIA (CONT'D)

John, I've had more than twenty years to ponder the matter that separated us, and I came to understand that you were a victim of a social injustice that has impeded the progress of our nation for years.

JOHN

And the sad thing, is that people's bigotry, hatred and racial prejudice blindly make them think and feel that they are right!

PATRICIA

You're right. And that's where we must come in! But the sad thing about it is that bigotry, hatred and prejudice are passed on by precept and example.

JOHN

The "Sixty Four Thousand Dollar Question" we must ask ourselves and the answer Pat is: "Where do we go from here?"

PATRICIA

John, with God's guidance, our hearts will let us know.

The scene closes and opens and John is walking into RaMon's Office and says –

JOHN

RaMon, guess what?

RaMon smiles and remarks –

RAMON

Yes, I know! I saw Pat in Ahmad's Office and later saw you go in there.

JOHN

You have known all this time who Ahmad is!

RAMON

Yes, I have!

JOHN

Well, why on earth didn't you tell me?

RAMON

I didn't feel that it was my business to tell you.

JOHN

Supposed I had rejected his application for CEO of our origination here in Robinsville?

RAMON

John, you were not employing your son, you were employing a man who can do the job. And knowing your son might have prejudiced your views.

JOHN

Which way?

RAMON

We will never know! But one thing is for certain, he likes you a lot and admires you.

JOHN

Yes, he likes me and admires me as a man and as his boss, but once he knows the facts, will he like me and admire me as a man and a father?

RAMON

Can't say for certain, but I have a strong and very strong feeling that he will!

The scene closes and opens and Ahmad (J.J.) is returning to his office.

J.J.

Mama, hope I didn't keep you waiting and you got bored.

With a glow in her eyes, Pat says –

PATRICIA

J.J., do you still believe in Fairy Tales?

J.J.

Well, mama, you told me so many that it's hard for me not to believe in them a little!

PATRICIA

Well, I do, too!

J.J. is making a few notes; putting his desk in order says –

J.J.

Did anybody drop by while I was out?

PATRICIA

Oh, yes, your Boss, Mr. Smith, dropped by.

J.J.

Oh, good. Then you two got to meet each other! What do you think of him?

PATRICIA

He's everything you said he is.

J.J.

If you get to know him, I'm sure that you would like him – he's a wonderful guy! Don't you think so, mom?

PATRICIA

Yes, he always was!

THE END

Made in the USA
Charleston, SC
30 July 2014